D1239537

ANATOMY
FOR STRENGTH AND FITNESS TRAINING
FOR SPEED

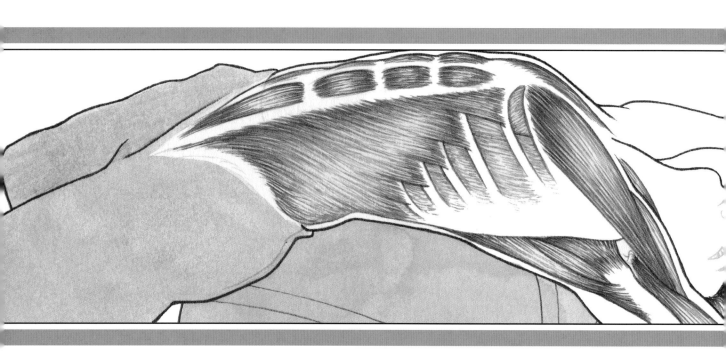

ANATOMY

FOR STRENGTH AND FITNESS TRAINING

FOR SPEED

LEIGH BRANDON

New York   Chicago   San Francisco   Lisbon   London
Madrid   Mexico City   Milan   New Delhi   San Juan
Seoul   Singapore   Sydney   Toronto

CONTENTS

PART 1. OVERVIEW OF ANATOMY

· How to Use This Book 6
  · Anatomical Definitions and Terminology 8
    · Systems of the Body 10
    · Body Planes and Regions 15
· Anatomical Terms 16
· Joint Movements 17
· Posture and Muscle Balance 21
· Preparation for Speed Training 23

PART 2. THE EXERCISES

1. Stretching and Warm-up 24

· **Mobilizations**
· Cervical/Thoracic 25
· Thoracic 26
· Lumbar 27
  · **Stretches**
  · Neck extensors 28
  · Neck side flexors 29
  · Pectoralis minor 30
  · Obliques 31
  · Abdominals 32

· Lumbar rotations 33
· Tensor fascia lata 34
· Hip flexors 35
· Adductors 36
· Hamstrings 37
· Calves 38
· **Pre-event Stretching**
· Squat push press 39
· Standing torso rotations 40
· Bend and reach 41
· Walking hamstring stretch 42
· Multi-directional lunges 43
· Walking arm swings 44
· Side shuffle 45
· Knee-ups 46
· Heel kicks 47

2. "The Core" 48
· Anatomy of the Core—Inner Unit 48
· **Exercises for the Inner Unit**
· Four-point tummy vacuum 50
· Horse stance—vertical 51
· Horse stance—horizontal 52
· Anatomy of the Core—Outer Unit 53

3. Primal Pattern® Movements 55
· Gait, Lunge, Squat, Bend, Pull, Push, Twis

4. Strength and Power 79
· Maximal Strength Training 80
· Power Training 86

5. Agility, Plyometrics, and Speed
· **Agility 92**
   Agility Drills: Hexagon drill, 180°
turn ladder drill, Zig-zag crossover
shuffle ladder drill, "A" movement
cone drill, "Z" pattern run cone
drill, "X" pattern multi-run cone
drill, square cone drill,
back-pedal forward,
lateral shuffle

· **Plyometrics 102**
   Plyometric Drills: Standing jump
and reach, 5-5-5 squat jump, Two-footed
jumps ladder drill, Side-to-side box
shuffle, Alternate bounding with single
arm action, Single leg bounding, Front
box jump, Jump from box, Depth jump

· **Speed 112**
   Speed Drills: Ankling, Butt kickers,
Ladder speed run, Ladder stride
run, Hurdle fast legs, Single leg hurdle
run-through, Hurdle run-
through, Falling starts,
Ankling to sprint, Hurdle run-
through to sprint, Ankling to
hurdle run-through to sprint

**PART 3. THE
PROGRAM**
· Designing Your
  Program 124
· Needs Analysis 125
· Goal Setting 125
· Strength Qualities 126
· Biomotor Abilities 127
· Movement Pattern
  Analysis 128
· Energy System
  Requirements 128
· Reflex Profiling 130
· Open- Versus Closed-
  Chain Exercises 131
· Periodization 132

References 134
Glossary 135
Index 136
Resources 143

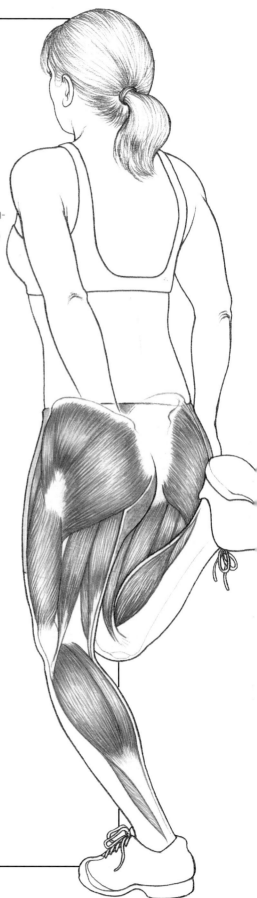

HOW TO USE THIS BOOK

Anatomy for Strength and Fitness Training for Speed and Sport is a visual, anatomical, and textual analysis of effective exercises that will help you in your chosen sporting field. It is also a guide on how to do the exercises, and how to safely and effectively develop speed for your particular sport. The book has three distinct parts: part one is a basic introduction to anatomical definitions, terminology, and an overview of the development of speed. Essentially, it helps to demystify the language used in part two, making it easier to follow the instructions in that part of the book.

Part two contains five sections: section one covers stretching and warm-up; section two covers "the core;" section three covers Primal Pattern® Movements; section four covers maximal strength and power development; and section five covers agility, plyometric, and speed drills. Within each section, the individual exercises or drills featured are defined and given some background. There is a "how-to" guide for doing the exercise, as well as a visual and technical exercise analysis of the main muscles that are working. The starting or finishing position is usually depicted and training tips may be included.

Part three helps you to understand how you might put these exercises together into a program over a season to achieve optimal speed and performance.

The adult human body has 639 muscles and 206 bones; this book illustrates approximately 92 muscles involved in movement and stabilization. Many smaller muscles, including the deep, small muscles of the spine and jaw and most muscles of the hands and feet are not given specific attention, in order not to confuse the reader.

This book has been designed to help you to improve your speed in your chosen sport. Before introducing speed training, the body has to be prepared to handle the loads or stresses put on the body during such training. Therefore, it is advised that the sections are completed in the following order:

1. **Primal Pattern® Movement beginner exercises**
2. **Primal Pattern® Movement intermediate exercises**
3. **Primal Pattern® Movement advanced exercises**
4. **Maximal strength training**
5. **Power training**
6. **Speed/agility/plyometric drills**

The length of time spent in each phase is dependent on your level of training experience. The more experience you have in training and the stronger you are, the less amount of time you need to spend in each phase. It is advised that you should have one to two years of resistance training before commencing "maximal strength" training.

Many of the exercises have a degree of risk of injury if done without adequate instruction and supervision. We recommend that you have a thorough assessment with a certified strength and conditioning coach, C.H.E.K practitioner or personal trainer before undertaking any of the exercises, and that you seek qualified instruction if you are a complete beginner. This book does not constitute medical advice, and the author and publisher cannot be held liable for any loss, injury, or inconvenience sustained by anyone using this book or the information contained in it.

Exercise name

How to start or finish the exercise, as shown in the small artwork

Essential training guidelines

Labels for the major muscles being used during the exercise

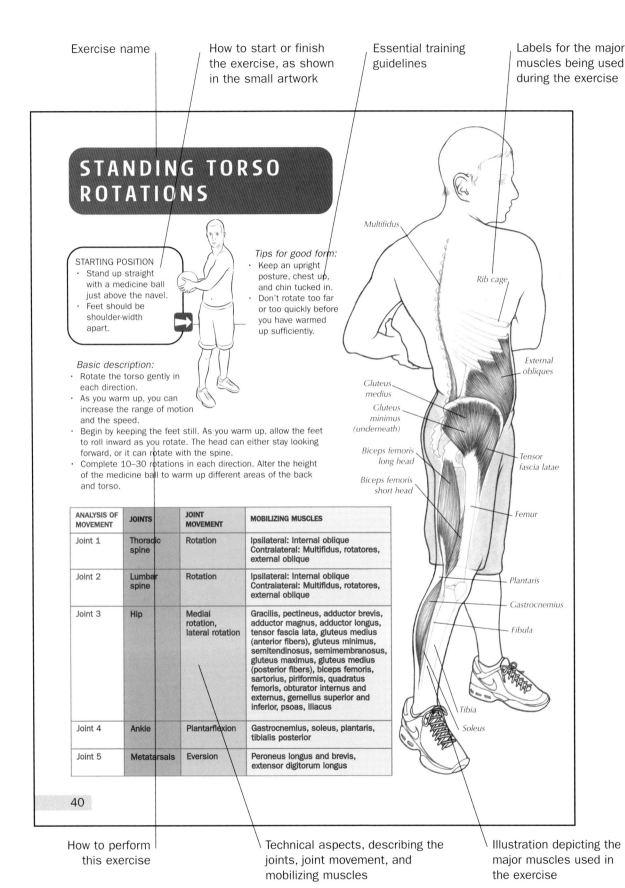

STANDING TORSO ROTATIONS

STARTING POSITION
· Stand up straight with a medicine ball just above the navel.
· Feet should be shoulder-width apart.

Tips for good form:
· Keep an upright posture, chest up, and chin tucked in.
· Don't rotate too far or too quickly before you have warmed up sufficiently.

Basic description:
· Rotate the torso gently in each direction.
· As you warm up, you can increase the range of motion and the speed.
· Begin by keeping the feet still. As you warm up, allow the feet to roll inward as you rotate. The head can either stay looking forward, or it can rotate with the spine.
· Complete 10–30 rotations in each direction. Alter the height of the medicine ball to warm up different areas of the back and torso.

Multifidus

Rib cage

External obliques

Gluteus medius

Gluteus minimus (underneath)

Biceps femoris long head

Biceps femoris short head

Tensor fascia latae

Femur

Plantaris

Gastrocnemius

Fibula

Tibia

Soleus

ANALYSIS OF MOVEMENT	JOINTS	JOINT MOVEMENT	MOBILIZING MUSCLES
Joint 1	Thoracic spine	Rotation	Ipsilateral: Internal oblique Contralateral: Multifidus, rotatores, external oblique
Joint 2	Lumbar spine	Rotation	Ipsilateral: Internal oblique Contralateral: Multifidus, rotatores, external oblique
Joint 3	Hip	Medial rotation, lateral rotation	Gracilis, pectineus, adductor brevis, adductor magnus, adductor longus, tensor fascia lata, gluteus medius (anterior fibers), gluteus minimus, semitendinosus, semimembranosus, gluteus maximus, gluteus medius (posterior fibers), biceps femoris, sartorius, piriformis, quadratus femoris, obturator internus and externus, gemellus superior and inferior, psoas, iliacus
Joint 4	Ankle	Plantarflexion	Gastrocnemius, soleus, plantaris, tibialis posterior
Joint 5	Metatarsals	Eversion	Peroneus longus and brevis, extensor digitorum longus

40

How to perform this exercise

Technical aspects, describing the joints, joint movement, and mobilizing muscles

Illustration depicting the major muscles used in the exercise

ANATOMICAL DEFINITIONS AND TERMINOLOGY

Anatomy has its own language and, while technical, it has a basis in logic, originating from Latin and Greek root words, that make it easier to learn and understand the names of muscles, bones, and other body parts.

Whether you're an athlete, personal trainer, or strength and conditioning coach, using the correct terminology enables you to interact with other professionals and professional materials.

Like most medical terms, anatomical terms are made up of small word parts, known as combining forms, that fit together to make the full term. These "combining forms" comprise roots, prefixes, and suffixes. Knowing the different word parts allows you to unravel the word. Most anatomical terms only contain two parts: either a prefix and a root, or a root and a suffix.

For example, if you take the terms subscapular and suprascapular, the root is "scapula," commonly known as the shoulder blade. "Supra" means "above," hence "suprascapula" means something above the shoulder blade; and "sub" means "below," indicating in this instance something below the shoulder blade.

Common prefixes, suffixes, and roots of anatomical terms

Word roots	Meaning	Example	Definition
abdomin	pertaining to the abdomen	abdominal muscle	major muscle group of the abdominal region
acro	extremity	acromion	protruding feature on the scapula bone
articul	pertaining to the joint	articular surface	joint surface
brachi	arm, pertaining to the arm	brachialis	arm muscle
cerv	neck, pertaining to the neck	cervical vertebrae	found in the neck region of the spine
crani	skull	cranium	bones forming the skull
glute	buttock	gluteus maximus	buttock muscle
lig	to tie, to bind	ligament	joins bone to bone
pect, pector	breast, chest	pectoralis major	chest muscle
Word parts used as prefixes			
ab-	away from, from, off	abduction	movement, away from the mid-line
ad-	increase, adherence, toward	adduction	movement, toward the mid-line
ante-, antero-	before, in front	anterior	front aspect of the body
bi-	two, double	bicep brachii	two-headed arm muscle
circum-	around	circumduction	making arm circles
cleido-	the clavicle	sternocleiomastoid	muscle, inserts into clavicle
con-	with, together	concentric contraction	contraction in which muscle attachments move together

Word parts used as prefixes (continued)

Word roots	Meaning	Example	Definition
costo-	rib	costal cartilages	rib cartilages
cune-	wedge	cuneiform	wedge-shaped foot bone
de-	down from, away from, undoing	depression	downward movement of the shoulder blades
dors-	back	dorsiflexion	movement where the "back" or topside of the foot raises up toward the shin
ec-	away from, out of	eccentric contractions	contraction in which muscle attachments move apart
epi-	upon	epicondyle	feature on a bone, located above a condyle
fasci-	band	tensor fascia late	small band-like muscle of the hip
flect-, flex-	bend	flexion	movement, closing the angle of a joint
infra-	below, beneath	infraspinatus muscle	situated below the spine (ridge) of the scapula
meta-	after, behind	metatarsals	bones of the foot, next to the tarsals
post-	after, behind	posterior	rear aspect of the body
pron-	bent forward	prone position	lying face down
proximo-	nearest	proximal	directional term, meaning nearest the root of a limb
quadr-	four	quadricep muscle	four-part muscle of the upper thigh
re-	back, again	retraction	movement, pulling the shoulder blades toward the mid-line
serrat-	saw	serratus anterior	muscle with a saw-like edge
sub-	beneath, inferior	subscapularis	muscle beneath the scapula
super-, supra-	over, above, excessive	supraspinatus muscle	featured above the spine (ridge) of the scapula
		superior	toward the head
thoraco-	the chest, thorax	thoracic vertebra	in the region of the thorax
trans-	across	transverse abdominus	muscle going across the abdomen, i.e. in the horizontal plane
tri-	three	tricep brachii	three-headed arm muscle
tuber-	swelling	tubercle	small rounded projection on a bone

Word parts used as suffixes

-al, -ac	pertaining to	iliac crest	pertaining to the ilium
-cep	head	bicep brachii	two-headed arm muscle
-ic	pertaining to	thoracic vertebra	pertaining to the thorax
-oid	like, in the shape of	rhomboid	upper back muscle, in the shape of a rhomboid
-phragm	partition	diaphragm	muscle separating the thorax and abdomen

The human body can be viewed as an integration of approximately 12 distinct systems that continuously interact to control a multitude of complex functions. These systems are a co-ordinated assembly of organs, each with specific capabilities, whose tissue structures suit a similar purpose and function.

This book illustrates and analyzes the systems that control movement and posture—namely the muscular and skeletal systems, often referred to jointly as the musculoskeletal system.

The other systems are the cardiovascular, lymphatic, nervous, endocrine, integumentary, respiratory, digestive, urinary, immune, and reproductive systems.

The muscular system

The muscular system facilitates movement, the maintenance of posture, and the production of heat and energy. This is made up of three types of muscle tissue: cardiac, smooth, and striated.

Cardiac muscle forms the heart walls, while smooth muscle tissue is found in the walls of internal organs such as the stomach and in blood vessels. Both types of muscle are activated involuntarily via the autonomic nervous system and hormonal action.

Striated muscle makes up the bulk of the muscles as we commonly know them. The skeletal system includes the tendons that attach muscle to bone, as well as the connective tissue that surrounds the muscle tissue which is called fascia. A human male weighing 154 lbs (70 kg) has approximately 55–77 lbs (25–35 kg) of skeletal muscle.

Muscle attachments

Muscles attach to bone via tendons. The attachment points are referred to as the origin and the insertion.

The origin is the point of attachment that is proximal (closest to the root of a limb) or closest to the mid-line (or center) of the body. It is usually the least moveable point, acting as the anchor in muscle contraction.

The insertion is the point of attachment that is distal (farthest from the root of a limb) or farthest from the mid-line or center of the body. The insertion is usually the most moveable part, and can be drawn toward the origin.

Knowing the origin and insertion of a muscle, which joint or joints the muscle crosses, and what movement is caused at that joint/joints is a key element of exercise analysis.

There are typical features on all bones that act as convenient attachment points for the muscles. A description of typical bone features is given in the table on page 13.

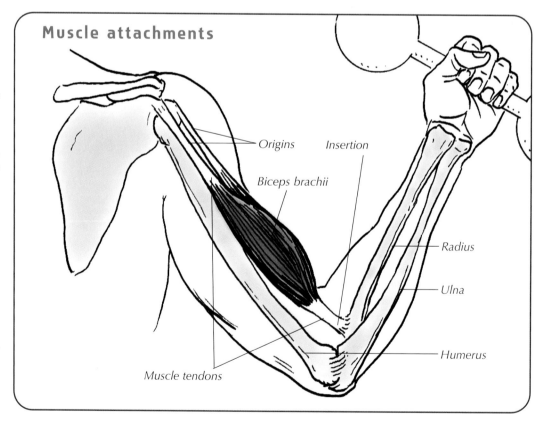

Muscle attachments

Origins   Insertion

Biceps brachii

Radius

Ulna

Humerus

Muscle tendons

The muscular system

Anterior view

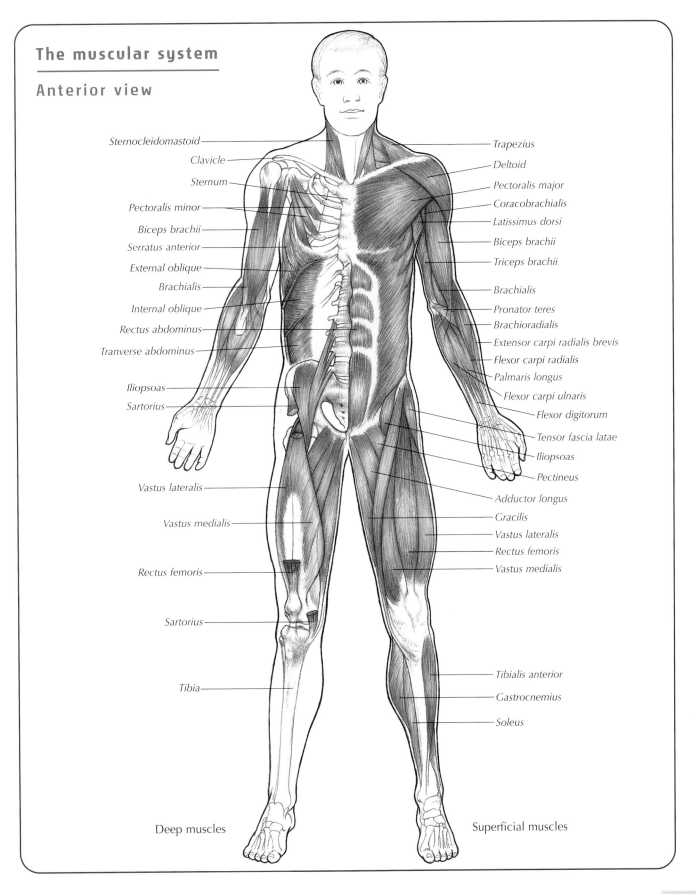

Sternocleidomastoid
Clavicle
Sternum
Pectoralis minor
Biceps brachii
Serratus anterior
External oblique
Brachialis
Internal oblique
Rectus abdominus
Tranverse abdominus
Iliopsoas
Sartorius
Vastus lateralis
Vastus medialis
Rectus femoris
Sartorius
Tibia

Trapezius
Deltoid
Pectoralis major
Coracobrachialis
Latissimus dorsi
Biceps brachii
Triceps brachii
Brachialis
Pronator teres
Brachioradialis
Extensor carpi radialis brevis
Flexor carpi radialis
Palmaris longus
Flexor carpi ulnaris
Flexor digitorum
Tensor fascia latae
Iliopsoas
Pectineus
Adductor longus
Gracilis
Vastus lateralis
Rectus femoris
Vastus medialis
Tibialis anterior
Gastrocnemius
Soleus

Deep muscles

Superficial muscles

The muscular system

Posterior view

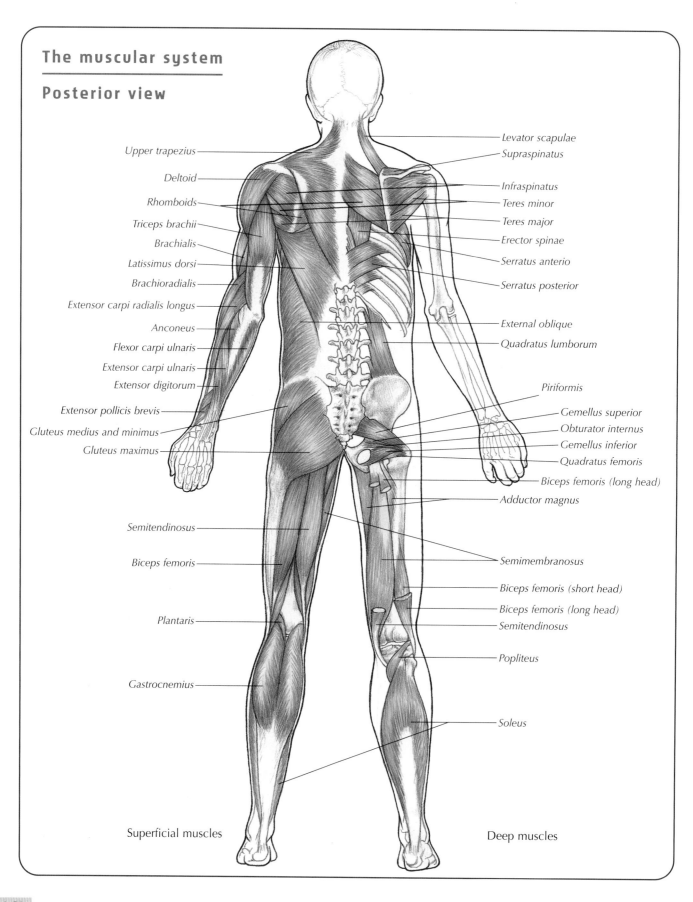

Upper trapezius

Deltoid

Rhomboids

Triceps brachii

Brachialis

Latissimus dorsi

Brachioradialis

Extensor carpi radialis longus

Anconeus

Flexor carpi ulnaris

Extensor carpi ulnaris

Extensor digitorum

Extensor pollicis brevis

Gluteus medius and minimus

Gluteus maximus

Semitendinosus

Biceps femoris

Plantaris

Gastrocnemius

Levator scapulae

Supraspinatus

Infraspinatus

Teres minor

Teres major

Erector spinae

Serratus anterio

Serratus posterior

External oblique

Quadratus lumborum

Piriformis

Gemellus superior

Obturator internus

Gemellus inferior

Quadratus femoris

Biceps femoris (long head)

Adductor magnus

Semimembranosus

Biceps femoris (short head)

Biceps femoris (long head)

Semitendinosus

Popliteus

Soleus

Superficial muscles

Deep muscles

Typical features on a bone

Feature	Description	Examples
Condyle	Large, rounded projection at a joint that usually articulates with another bone	· Medial and lateral condyle of the femur · Lateral condyle of the tibia
Epicondyle	Projection located above a condyle	Medial or lateral epicondyle of the humerus
Facet	Small, flat joint surfaces	Facet joints of the vertebrae
Head	Significant, rounded projection at the proximal end of a bone, usually forming a joint	Head of the humerus
Crest	Ridge-like, narrow projection	Iliac crest of the pelvis
Line, Linea	Lesser significant ridge, running along a bone	Linea aspera of the femur
Process	Any significant projection	· Coracoid and acromion process of the scapula · Olecranon process of the ulna at the elbow joint
Spine, Spinous process	Significant, slender projection away from the surface of the bone	· Spinous processes of the vertebra · Spine of the scapula
Suture	Joint line between two bones forming a fixed or semi-fixed joint	Sutures that join the bones of the skull
Trochanter	Very large projection	Greater trochanter of the femur
Tubercle	Small, rounded projection	Greater tubercles of the humerus
Tuberosity	Large, rounded, or roughened projection	Ischial tuberosities on the pelvis, commonly known as the "sitting bones"
Foramen	Rounded hole or opening in a bone	The vertebral foramen running down the length of the spine, in which the spinal cord is housed
Fossa	Hollow, shallow, or flattened surface on a bone	Supraspinous and infraspinous fossa on the scapula

The word "skeleton" originates from a Greek word meaning "dried up." Infants are born with about 350 bones, many of which fuse as they grow, forming single bones, resulting in the 206 bones found in an adult.

The skeletal system

This consists of bones, ligaments (that join bone to bone), and joints. Joints are referred to as articulations and are sometimes classified as a separate system: the articular system.

Apart from facilitating movement, the primary functions of the skeletal system include supporting the muscles, protecting the soft tissues and internal organs, the storage of surplus minerals, and the formation of red blood cells in the bone marrow of the long bones.

Integrated systems

The body's systems are completely and intricately interdependent. For movement to take place, for example, the respiratory system brings in oxygen and the digestive system breaks down our food into essential nutrients, both of which the cardiovascular system then carries to the working muscles via the blood to facilitate the energy reactions that result in physical work being done.

The lymphatic and circulatory systems help to carry away the waste products of these energy reactions, which are later converted and/or excreted by the digestive and urinary systems. The nervous system interacts with the muscles to facilitate the contraction and relaxation of the muscle tissue. The articular system of joints allows the levers of the body to move.

The femur (thigh bone) is about one-quarter of a person's height. It is also the largest, heaviest, and strongest bone in the body. The shortest bone, the stirrup bone in the ear, is only about 2.5 mm long. An adult's skeleton weighs about 20 lb (9 kg).

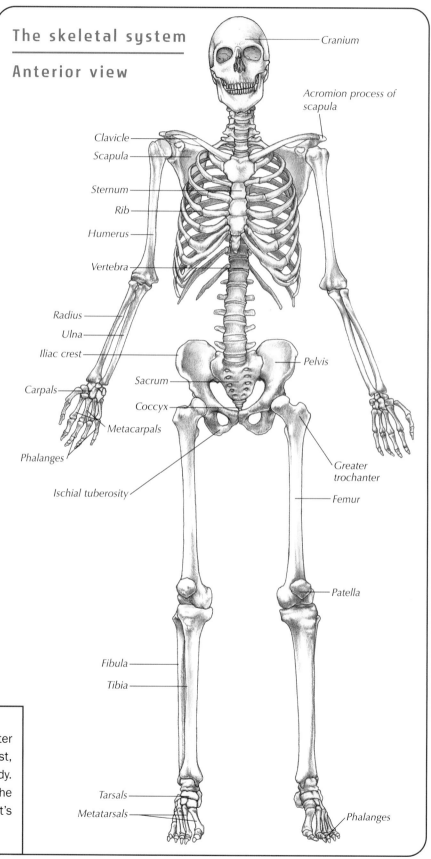

The skeletal system

Anterior view

- Cranium
- Acromion process of scapula
- Clavicle
- Scapula
- Sternum
- Rib
- Humerus
- Vertebra
- Radius
- Ulna
- Iliac crest
- Pelvis
- Carpals
- Sacrum
- Coccyx
- Metacarpals
- Phalanges
- Greater trochanter
- Ischial tuberosity
- Femur
- Patella
- Fibula
- Tibia
- Tarsals
- Metatarsals
- Phalanges

BODY PLANES AND REGIONS

When learning anatomy and analyzing movement, we refer to a standard reference position of the human body, known as the anatomical position. All movements and locations of anatomical structures are named as if the person was standing in this position (see illustrations below).

Regional anatomy

This book is a technical labeling guide to the different superficial parts of the body. In anatomical language, common names such as "head" are replaced with anatomical terms derived from Latin, such as cranial or cranium.

Within the different body regions there are subregions. For example, within the cranial region are the frontal, occipital, parietal, and temporal subregions.

Anatomical planes

The body can be divided into three imaginary planes of reference, each perpendicular to the other (see illustration below).

The sagittal plane passes through the body from front to back, dividing it into a right half and a left half. The mid-line of the body is called the median. If the body is divided in the sagittal plane, directly through its median, this is known as the median sagittal plane. The coronal (frontal plane) passes through the body from top to bottom, dividing it into front and back sections.

The transverse (horizontal) plane passes through the middle of the body at right angles, dividing it into top and bottom sections.

An anatomical cross-section of the internal structures of the body can be viewed in any one of these planes, which are also described as "planes of motion," as the joint movements are defined in relation to one of the three planes. Understanding into which plane an anatomical cross-section is divided will help you to know what you are looking at and from which viewpoint.

Anatomical position

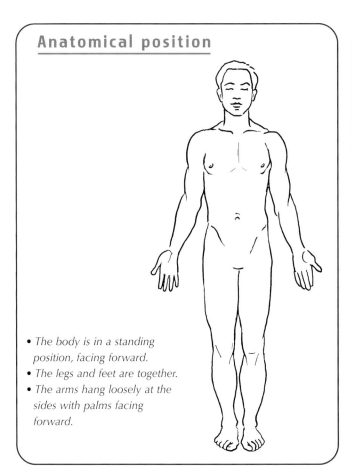

- *The body is in a standing position, facing forward.*
- *The legs and feet are together.*
- *The arms hang loosely at the sides with palms facing forward.*

Anatomical planes

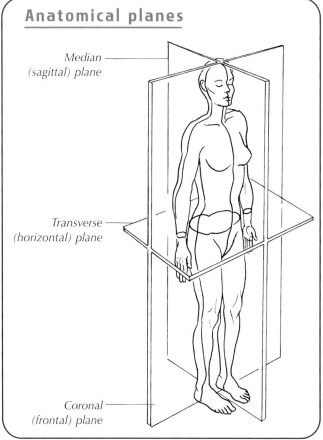

Median (sagittal) plane

Transverse (horizontal) plane

Coronal (frontal) plane

ANATOMICAL TERMS

There are standard anatomical terms that describe the position or direction of one structure of the body and its relationship to other structures or parts of the body.

The human body is a complex, three-dimensional structure; knowing the proper anatomical terms of position and direction will help you to compare one point on the body with another, and understand where it is situated in relation to other anatomical features.

These terms are standard, no matter whether the person is standing, seated, or lying down, and are named as if the person was standing in the anatomical position (see page 15). The terms of direction should not be confused with joint movements (see pages 17–20).

Anatomical terms of position and direction

Position	Definition	Example of usage
Anterior	Toward the front, pertaining to the front	The pectoral muscles are found on the anterior aspect of the body
Posterior	Toward the back, pertaining to the rear	The calf muscles are situated on the posterior surface of the lower leg
Superior	Above another structure, toward the head	The knee is superior to the ankle
Inferior	Below another structure, toward the feet	The hip is inferior to the shoulder
Lateral	Away from the mid-line, on or toward the outside	The radial bone is lateral to the ulna
Medial	Toward the mid-line of the body, pertaining to the middle or center	The tibial bone is medial to the fibula
Proximal	Closest to the trunk or root of a limb. Also sometimes used to refer to the origin of a muscle	The shoulder joint is proximal to the elbow
Distal	Situated away from the mid-line or center of the body, or root of a limb. Also sometimes used to refer to a point away from the origin of a muscle	The knee joint is distal to the hip
Superficial	Closer to the surface of the body, more toward the surface of the body than another structure	The rectus abdominus is the most superficial muscle of the abdominal wall
Deep	Farther from the surface, relatively deeper into the body than another structure	The transverse abdominus is the deepest muscle of the abdominal wall
Prone	Lying face downward	The lumbar mobilization (see page 27) begins in a prone position
Supine	Lying on the back, face upward	The bench press exercise (see page 84) is performed from a supine position

JOINT MOVEMENTS

Knowing and understanding movement (which joint is moving, how it moves) is essential to being able to analyze a complex exercise. This book has done the job of joint identification for you, and understanding this section will help to improve your exercise analysis.

Types of joints
Some joints are fixed or semi-fixed, allowing little or no movement. For instance, the bones of the skull join together in structures known as sutures to form fixed joints. But when the spine joins the pelvis, the sacroiliac joint is semi-fixed and allows minimal movement ("sacro" from sacrum and "iliac" pertaining to the ilium of the pelvis).

A third category called synovial joints are free-moving and move in different ways determined by their particular shape, size, and structure.

Synovial joints are the most common joints in the body. They are categorized by a joint capsule that surrounds the articulation, the inner membrane of which secretes lubricating synovial fluid, stimulated by movement. Typical synovial joints include the shoulder, knee, hip, ankle, joints of the feet and hands, and the vertebral joints.

Joint action
When performing an activity such as lifting weights or running, the combination of nerve stimulation and muscular contraction facilitates the movement that occurs at the synovial joints.

When doing a squat, for example (see page 62), the body weight rises away from the floor, because the angle of the ankle, knee, and hip joints increases due to the muscles acting across the joints, contracting and causing the joints to extend.

Joint movement pointers
Most joint movements have common names that apply to most major joints, but there are some movements that occur at only one specific joint.

The common joint movements occur in similar anatomical planes of motion. For example, shoulder, hip, and knee flexion all occur in the sagittal plane (see page 15). This makes it easier to learn about joint movements and movement analysis.

In the table below, common movements are listed first, followed by specific movements that only occur at one joint.

Strictly speaking, it is incorrect to name only the movement and a limb or body part. For example, "leg extension" does not clarify whether this happens at the knee, hip, or ankle. Get into the habit of always pairing the movement with the joint that is moved—elbow flexion, hip extension, spinal rotation, and scapular elevation. (Possibly the only exception to this is when referring to trunk movements, when all the joints of the spine combine to create movement of the whole body part).

Movements generally occur in pairs. For every movement, there must be a return movement to the starting position. Typical pairs are flexion and extension, abduction and adduction, internal rotation and external rotation, protraction and retraction, elevation and depression.

Remember, all movements are named as if the person was standing in the anatomical position (see page 15). So "elbow flexion" is the same regardless of whether you are standing, seated, or lying down.

Major joint movements

General movements	Plane	Description	Example
Abduction	Coronal	Movement away from the mid-line	Hip abduction (see page 45)
Adduction	Coronal	Movement toward the mid-line	Hip adduction (see page 45)
Flexion	Sagittal	Decreasing the angle between two structures	Knee flexion during the squat (see page 62)
Extension	Sagittal	Increasing the angle between two structures	Knee extension during the squat (see page 62)
Medial rotation (internal rotation)	Transverse	Turning around the vertical axis of a bone toward the mid-line	Return of the bar to the floor following completion of the power clean (see page 88)

Lateral rotation (external/ outward rotation)	Transverse	Turning around the vertical axis of a bone away from the mid-line	Shoulder lateral rotation during second pull on the power clean (see page 88)
Circumduction	All planes	Complete circular movement at shoulder or hip joints	Walking arm swings (see page 44)

Specific movements

1. Ankle movements

Plantarflexion	Sagittal	Moving the toes downward	Depth jumps (see page 111)
Dorsiflexion (dorsal flexion)	Sagittal	Moving the foot toward the shin	Depth jumps (see page 111)

2. Forearm movements (the radioulnar joint)

Pronation	Transverse	Rotating the hand and wrist medially from the elbow	Single arm cable push (see page 73)
Supination	Transverse	Rotating the hand and wrist laterally from the elbow	Single arm cable pull (see pages 68–69)

3. Scapula movements

Depression	Coronal	Movement of the scapulae inferiorly, e.g. squeezing scapulae downward	Chin-up (see page 83)
Elevation	Coronal	Movement of the scapulae superiorly, e.g. hunching the shoulders	Power clean (see page 88)
Abduction (protraction)	Transverse	Movement of the scapulae away from the spine	Bench press (see page 84)
Adduction (retraction)	Transverse	Movement of the scapulae toward the spine	Deadlift (see page 82)
Downward rotation (medial rotation)	Coronal	Scapulae rotate downward, in the return from the upward rotation	The pull on the chin-up (see page 83)
Upward rotation (lateral rotation)	Coronal	Scapulae rotate upward.The inferior angle of the scapula moves upward and laterally	The return on the chin-up (see page 83)

4. Shoulder movements

Horizontal abduction/extension (transverse abduction)	Transverse	Movement of the humerus across the body away from the mid-line	Single arm cable push (see page 73)
Horizontal adduction/flexion (transverse adduction)	Transverse	Movement of the humerus across the body toward the mid-line	Single arm cable pull (see pages 68–69)

5. Spine/trunk movements

Lateral flexion	Coronal	Movement of the trunk away from the mid-line	Obliques stretch (see page 31)
Reduction (adduction/return)	Coronal	Return of the trunk toward the mid-line in the coronal plane	Obliques stretch (see page 31)

6. Wrist movements

Ulnar deviation	Coronal	Movement of the hand toward the mid-line from the anatomical position	When banging a hammer
Radial deviation	Coronal	Movement of the hand away from the mid-line from the anatomical position	When banging a hammer

Joint movements

The knee joint is the largest, the hip joint is the strongest, and the shoulder is potentially the most unstable joint in the body.

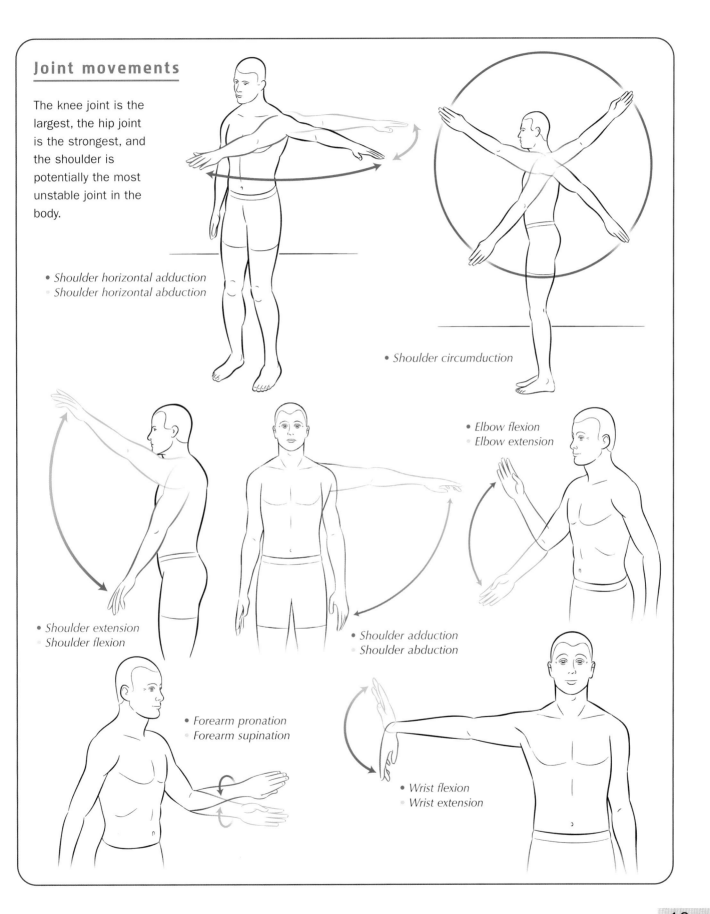

- *Shoulder horizontal adduction*
- *Shoulder horizontal abduction*

- *Shoulder circumduction*

- *Shoulder extension*
- *Shoulder flexion*

- *Elbow flexion*
- *Elbow extension*

- *Shoulder adduction*
- *Shoulder abduction*

- *Forearm pronation*
- *Forearm supination*

- *Wrist flexion*
- *Wrist extension*

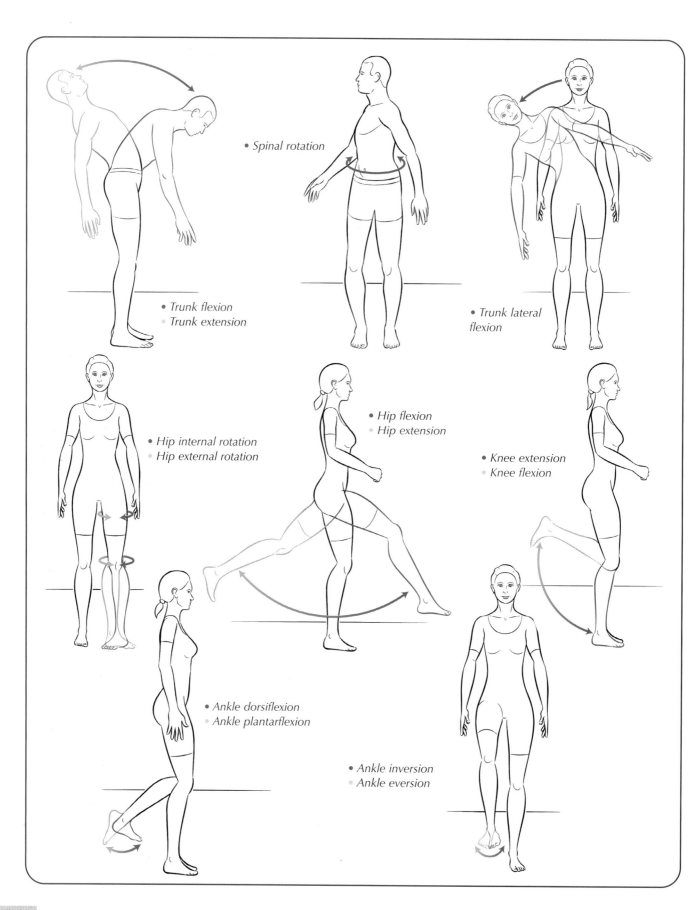

- *Spinal rotation*

- *Trunk flexion*
- *Trunk extension*

- *Trunk lateral flexion*

- *Hip internal rotation*
- *Hip external rotation*

- *Hip flexion*
- *Hip extension*

- *Knee extension*
- *Knee flexion*

- *Ankle dorsiflexion*
- *Ankle plantarflexion*

- *Ankle inversion*
- *Ankle eversion*

POSTURE AND MUSCLE BALANCE

Posture has become quite a buzz word in recent years. However, the understanding, importance, and methods of correcting posture are often misunderstood.

There are many definitions of posture. Two include:

"Posture is the position from which all movement begins and ends." (P. Chek, *CHEK Golf Biomechanic Certification Manual*)

"The position from which the musculoskeletal system functions most efficiently." (M. Feldenkrais, *Body and Mature Behavior*)

In addition to the definitions above, there are two main categories of posture: static and dynamic.

Static posture

Static posture may be defined as "...the position of the body at rest, sitting, standing or lying" (P. Chek, *CHEK Golf Biomechanic Certification Manual*). This means that if you have poor posture before you move, you are more likely to have poor posture while moving. Therefore, poor static posture could well be expressed in your movements.

Dynamic posture

Dynamic posture may be defined as "the ability to maintain an optimal instantaneous axis of rotation in any combination of movement planes at any time in space" (P. Chek, *CHEK Golf Biomechanic Certification Manual*). As a simple analogy, you can think of your spine as an axis of rotation (like a crankshaft), and your arms as a means by which motion at the axis is expressed (like the connecting rod). If your spinal axis is faulty and expresses the exaggerated curvatures that go hand in hand with poor posture, your capacity to rotate efficiently will be significantly reduced. If your spinal axis is well aligned, you are far more efficient and are likely to move and perform to your full potential.

Optimal posture is maintained when muscles surrounding a joint or joints are in balance. Good "muscle balance" simply means that the muscles are at their optimal or normal length and tension. A muscle imbalance is when a muscle on one side of a joint is tight and its opposing muscle (antagonist) is long and potentially weak. This causes the joint to lose its optimal axis of rotation, and can lead to excessive wear and tear on the joint, and increase the likelihood of injury during sports.

It is beyond the scope of this book to instruct you on how to maintain optimal posture and muscle balance. Instead, we would suggest that you receive advice from a qualified professional—or read *Anatomy of Yoga for Posture and Health* by Leigh Brandon and Nicky Jenkins (see page 144). It is also advised that you achieve the best possible muscle balance before beginning the exercises in this book.

Posture and alignment

The gravitational pull that is exerted on the body acts through the body in a straight line towards the earth's center. In a standing position, neutral alignment occurs when landmarks such as the ankles, knees, hips, shoulders, and ears are in line with the pull of gravity. The body also requires balance from front to back and side to side, allowing it to maintain its position against gravity with minimal effort. The more the body is out of alignment, the more energy it uses to resist the gravitational pull. For most athletes, poor posture could not only cause injury, but also waste vital energy, and could make the difference between winning and losing.

In neutral alignment, the pelvis is in a neutral position with the pubic ramus and the anterior superior iliac crest vertically aligned. In this position, if the pelvis was a bucket of water, no water would spill out. With an anterior pelvic tilt, the water would pour out the front, while a posterior pelvic tilt would cause the water to pour out the back.

As we exercise and move the body in different positions, such as squats or lunges, gravity continues to affect the body, the critical points of balance shift and we are required to work harder to maintain balance and alignment. When lifting heavy weights, despite the fact that your balance is shifting, in some instances it is still important to maintain a neutral spine. "Neutral spine" in the instance of performing squats would require the maintenance of a straight line through the ear, shoulder, pelvis, and hips, but not necessarily in a vertical line.

Poor postural control and alignment affect both your quality of movement and the safety and effectiveness of any exercise, as postural compensation is likely to occur. This means that the joints used, joint actions, range of movement, and involvement of the various stabilizing and mobilizing muscles will change from the ideal. For instance, in the squat, if you had a tight soleus (calf muscle) in the right leg, your body weight would shift to the right as you descended in the squat. This would place more stress through the medial left knee and lateral right knee.

Posture and alignment

One common classification of muscles is whether they are performing a stabilizing or mobilizing function.

A mobilizer muscle (also called a phasic muscle) is a muscle primarily responsible for creating movement across joints. For example, the gluteus maximus extending the hip joint during the lunge (see page 59).

Stabilizers (also known as tonic muscles) are muscles whose prime purpose in the body or in a given movement is to maintain the stability and alignment of the rest of the body, so that effective movement can be performed by the mobilizing muscles. For example, in the chin-up (see page 83), the rotator cuff muscles of the shoulder stabilize the shoulder joint as the latissimus dorsi and pectoralis major adduct the shoulder joint to pull the body up to the bar. Certain muscles, by virtue of their position, shape, angle, and muscle fiber type, are more suited to work as stabilizers than mobilizers. Stabilizing muscles tend to be deep in the joint, have lots of endurance, but can't produce much power. Mobilizer muscles tend to be more superficial, have little endurance, but can produce a lot of power.

An important yet controversial area of the body is the abdominal musculature, which is widely believed to help stabilize the body, particularly the lumbar spine, rib cage, and pelvis (which are the foundations for the arms and legs), but how it achieves this stability is not universally accepted (see pages 48–52).

Classifications of speed

Classification	Definition
Speed	Distance covered over time; time taken to complete task
Starting speed	The ability of a muscle to generate maximum force at the beginning of a movement
Acceleration	Rate of increase in velocity
Deceleration	Rate of decrease in velocity
Agility	A speedy change of direction involving a deceleration followed by an acceleration, in response to a stimulus in any direction, while maintaining balance
Reactive speed	The ability to switch from eccentric to concentric muscle contraction quickly
Maximal speed	Maximal top speed; flat-out speed
Lateral speed	Speed of movement in a sideways direction
Speed endurance	The ability to maintain speed over a distance

In sport, different events require different speed qualities. For instance, a 100 meter sprinter will require starting speed, acceleration, reactive speed, and maximal speed. However, a tennis player would require starting speed, acceleration, deceleration, agility, reactive speed, and lateral speed.

You will need to analyze your own sport and decide which speed qualities are vital. In team sports, you may also need to be more specific. For instance, the speed requirements may be different depending on which position you play or even your particular style of play.

For instance, a wide receiver in American football would need maximal speed where perhaps a lineman would not. A rugby winger would require maximal speed, but a volleyball player would not.

In many sports, particularly team games and ball sports, the speed of thought or anticipation is essential. Failure to anticipate your opponents' or team mates' movements, or the movement of the ball can be the difference between success and failure. While it is beyond the scope of this book, speed drills should be performed in competition-specific conditions once you have perfected your skill. This will allow you to develop speed of thought in competitive situations.

PREPARATION FOR SPEED TRAINING

As the illustration below shows, speed development is at the peak of performance. Before you get to the peak, you have to build a solid base. Over the years I have explained to my athletes and clients that to build a strong, powerful, quick body, you have to treat it like building a skyscraper.

Before you can construct any building, you need to build solid foundations. This is also true for developing a body that is required to move quickly. Buildings need to be able to withstand earthquakes, extreme weather, and other unforeseen stresses. Moving the human body at speed is similar to a building during an earthquake: it has to handle a lot of stress without breaking down.

With any building, the stronger the foundations, the taller and stronger it can be. The same is true for the athlete. A saying I find useful here is "the wider the base, the taller the peak." Therefore, it is important that a strong base of flexibility, stability, and movement skill is achieved before moving to maximal strength.

In some sports, it is advantageous to be very strong regardless of body weight. For instance, a shot putter or heavyweight boxer has no restrictions on body weight. However, some sports have weight categories or it is advantageous to be smaller, for instance if you're a figure skater or a jockey. An athlete who does not have to consider their weight requires "absolute strength," while an athlete who has to consider their body weight requires "relative strength." Relative strength means that the athlete has to maximize their strength without increasing body weight (see page 79).

Therefore, the athlete has to decide whether they require muscle hypertrophy as part of their base conditioning phase.

Beginners should spend the first one to two years developing their skill of movement and preparing their bodies for the higher levels of stress of maximal strength and speed development in order to reduce the likelihood of injury.

Lower intensity agility, plyometric, and speed drills can be used prior to maximal strength training (see table one on page 102). These exercises are a good introduction to this type of training. However, the development of true optimal speed will occur following maximal strength training and higher intensity agility, plyometric, and speed training.

To move the body quickly, you are required to generate as much force (peak force) as possible in the shortest possible time to move your body weight, and perhaps the weight of an implement, ball, or opponent. As peak force is required, the stronger you are, the more force you can generate. This is why maximal strength training is so crucial for power and speed development.

Maximal strength can then be followed by a combination of power, agility, plyometric, and speed drills to achieve optimal speed for your sport.

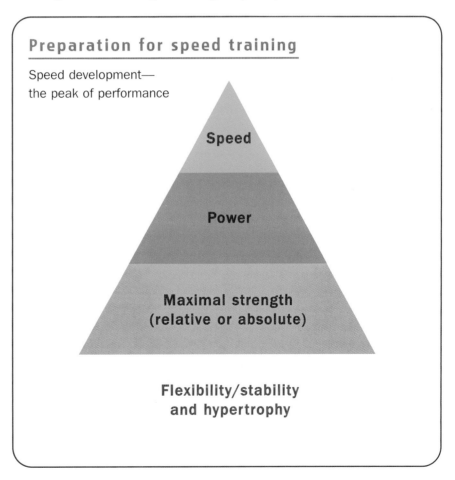

Preparation for speed training

Speed development—
the peak of performance

Speed

Power

Maximal strength
(relative or absolute)

**Flexibility/stability
and hypertrophy**

STRETCHING AND WARM-UP

There is a big debate as to whether you should stretch before and/or after exercise, and how you should warm up prior to workouts or competition.

There is evidence that suggests that stretching prior to exercise has no benefit and that it can even be detrimental to performance. There is some truth in these statements.

However, everything has to be put into context with each individual situation. As noted on pages 21 and 22, muscle balance and posture are crucial to optimizing performance and reducing the likelihood of injury. So here's my question: do you want to train or perform with tight muscles and therefore poor muscular balance? Quite clearly, no!

In rehabilitative, corrective, or base conditioning phases of your training plan, corrective mobilizations and stretches are used to lengthen the short, tight, and facilitated muscles in the body. These are normally the tonic muscles, but every individual is different. A simple way to check this is to perform each mobilization and stretch (see pages 25–38) and if you feel tightness or discomfort in the targeted area or muscle, add it to your mobilizing and stretching program. Ideally, you should seek a full assessment by a qualified professional, such as a C.H.E.K practitioner, physiotherapist, or strength and conditioning coach.

This pre-workout mobilization and stretching will allow the muscles to work through a wider range and for their antagonistic muscles to strengthen through a more optimal range.

As the training becomes more intensive and moves into maximal strength, power, or speed training, then this type of pre-stretching can be detrimental. If a muscle is stretched beyond its normal range or for too long, the nerve impulses that supply the muscles can be down-regulated. This means the muscles will produce less force. This is not ideal if you wish to train or perform close to your maximal effort and it may be dangerous in a contact sport when your opponent may then be able to generate more power than you, leaving you to crawl around the field searching for your teeth in the grass!

So to make this really clear, if you are doing exercises from pages 50–52 (inner unit) or 58–78 (Primal Pattern® Movement training), it is advised that you perform the mobilizations and stretches that are appropriate to you prior to your workouts in the gym. You should also warm-up by completing one or two sets of each exercise at 60–80 percent of your working intensity.

Prior to maximal strength, power, agility, plyometric, and speed workouts, the pre-event stretches and warm-ups (pages 39–47) should be performed. This is essential to prepare the bodily systems required prior to your workout or event to maximize your performance. By preparing the neuromuscular, cardiovascular, and respiratory systems, you will be ready to perform at your best while minimizing the likelihood of injury. This likelihood is reduced because when muscles are warm, the tissues are less viscous and able to move through a wider range of motion, and are therefore less likely to tear when moved at speed.

The warm-up exercises shown in this section are just a selection of some of the most commonly used in the field of sport. You should analyze the movement patterns of your sport or workout and use warm-up exercises that closely mimic those movements. You can also use your imagination to devise adaptations on those exercises given to better prepare you for specific workouts or for your sport.

As you warm up, you should slowly and gradually increase your speed until you reach speeds close to that of your sport. By the end of your warm-up you should have a light sweat, but you should not overdo the warm-up and waste vital energy.

If you are in a phase of maximal strength, power, or speed you should still perform corrective mobilizations and stretches. The only difference is when you perform them, which you can do as part of your post-event cool-down. This helps to remove metabolic waste from the muscles, and anecdotal evidence suggests (although research does not back this up) that stretching post-exercise helps to reduce muscle soreness. Metabolic waste continues to be produced for up to four hours after exercise, therefore post-exercise stretching is unlikely to maintain muscle length.

Another key time to stretch is before you go to bed. This allows the muscles to regenerate in their lengthened position (muscles regenerate when you are asleep, normally between 10 p.m. and 2 a.m. when growth hormone levels are optimal). Stretching before bed also helps to relax the mind and aid recovery.

MOBILIZATIONS

CERVICAL/THORACIC MOBILIZATION

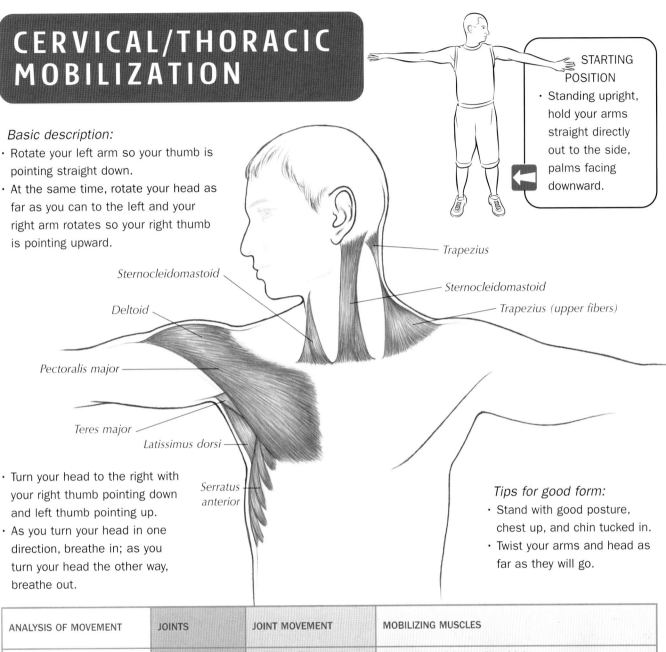

STARTING POSITION
· Standing upright, hold your arms straight directly out to the side, palms facing downward.

Basic description:
· Rotate your left arm so your thumb is pointing straight down.
· At the same time, rotate your head as far as you can to the left and your right arm rotates so your right thumb is pointing upward.

Trapezius

Sternocleidomastoid

Trapezius (upper fibers)

Sternocleidomastoid

Deltoid

Pectoralis major

Teres major

Latissimus dorsi

Serratus anterior

· Turn your head to the right with your right thumb pointing down and left thumb pointing up.
· As you turn your head in one direction, breathe in; as you turn your head the other way, breathe out.

Tips for good form:
· Stand with good posture, chest up, and chin tucked in.
· Twist your arms and head as far as they will go.

ANALYSIS OF MOVEMENT	JOINTS	JOINT MOVEMENT	MOBILIZING MUSCLES
Joint 1	Cervical spine	Rotation	Contralateral (opposite side): Trapezius (upper fibers), sternocleidomastoid, scalenes Ipsilateral (same side): Levator scapula, splenius capitis and cervicis, rectus capitis posterior major, oblique capitis inferior, longus coli, longus capitis
Joint 2	Shoulder	External rotation, internal rotation	Deltoid, infraspinatus, teres minor, latissimus dorsi, teres major, pectoralis major, subscapularis
Joint 3	Scapula	Mid and lower spinal extensors	Trapezius (middle fibers), rhomboids, serratus anterior, pectoralis minor

THORACIC MOBILIZATION

Basic description:
- Inhale, then as you exhale, slowly allow the upper spine to drop down toward the floor.
- Slowly rise back up, inhaling as you do so.
- Repeat this process three times. Then, move the foam roller one vertebra above (about an inch higher) and repeat another three times.
- Continue this process until you reach the spine of the scapula.

STARTING POSITION
- Lie on the floor with the foam roller placed across your back at the level of the base of the shoulder blades.
- Cup the back of your neck with your hands and place your tongue on the roof of your mouth behind the front teeth (anatomical position of the tongue).

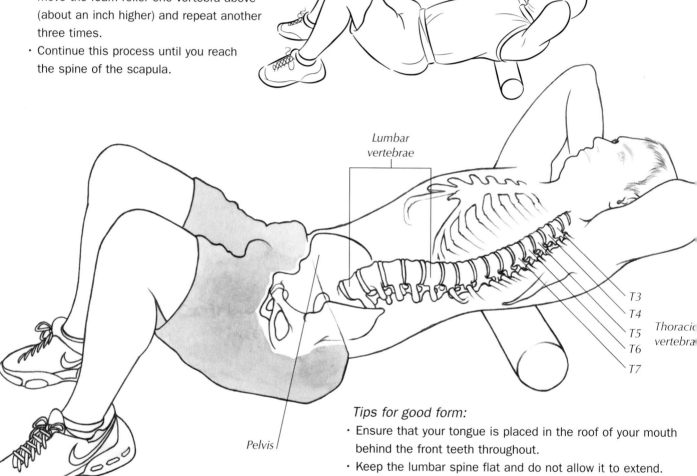

Lumbar vertebrae

T3
T4
T5   Thoracic
T6   vertebra
T7

Pelvis

Tips for good form:
- Ensure that your tongue is placed in the roof of your mouth behind the front teeth throughout.
- Keep the lumbar spine flat and do not allow it to extend.
- Keep hold of your neck, not your head. Holding the head will create shear forces through the neck.
- Move slowly.

ANALYSIS OF MOVEMENT	JOINTS	JOINT MOVEMENT	MOBILIZING JOINTS
Joint 1	Thoracic	Down: extension Up: flexion	T7–T3

LUMBAR MOBILIZATION

STARTING POSITION
· Lie face down (prone), elbows bent, and palms lying face down (pronated) next to the shoulders.

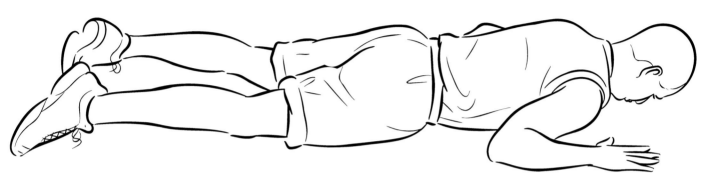

Basic description:
· Inhale, then as you exhale push through the arms, raise each vertebra one at a time from the top toward the bottom.
· Keep the front pelvic bones (anterior superior iliac spines) in contact with the ground.
· Go as far as you can without the pelvic bones leaving the floor, and return to the start position while inhaling.
· Try to move farther each time with good form.

Tips for good form:
· Keep the pelvic bones in contact with the ground.
· Keep the head in line with the spine (do not flex or extend the head or neck).

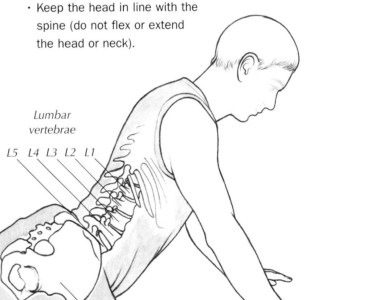

Lumbar
vertebrae

L5 L4 L3 L2 L1

Pelvis

ANALYSIS OF MOVEMENT	JOINTS	JOINT MOVEMENT	MOBILIZING JOINTS
Joint 1	Lumbar spine	Up: extension	L1–L5

Note: Anyone who experiences pain doing this mobilization should not continue performing it and should seek professional advice.

STRETCHES

NECK EXTENSORS

STARTING POSITION
· Start seated or standing with good posture.
· One hand on chin/lower jaw.

Basic description:

· Tuck your chin in toward the neck. You can use one hand to push and hold the chin inward.

· When you feel a stretch on the upper extensors on the back of the neck just below the back of the skull (occiput), place your other hand on the back of the head.

· Inhale, then push your head back into the hand with about 10 percent of maximum effort while holding your breath. Resist the movement of your head with your hand so there is no backward movement of the head.

· After contracting the muscles for five seconds, relax, exhale, and as you exhale, move the chin inward, and increase the stretch until you find a new position of "bind."

· Repeat this process three to five times.

Tips for good form:

· Keep your torso upright.
· Keep your chin tucked in.
· Keep your head still when you are contracting the muscles.

Splenius capitus (under trapezius)

Levator scalpulae

Trapezius (upper fibers)

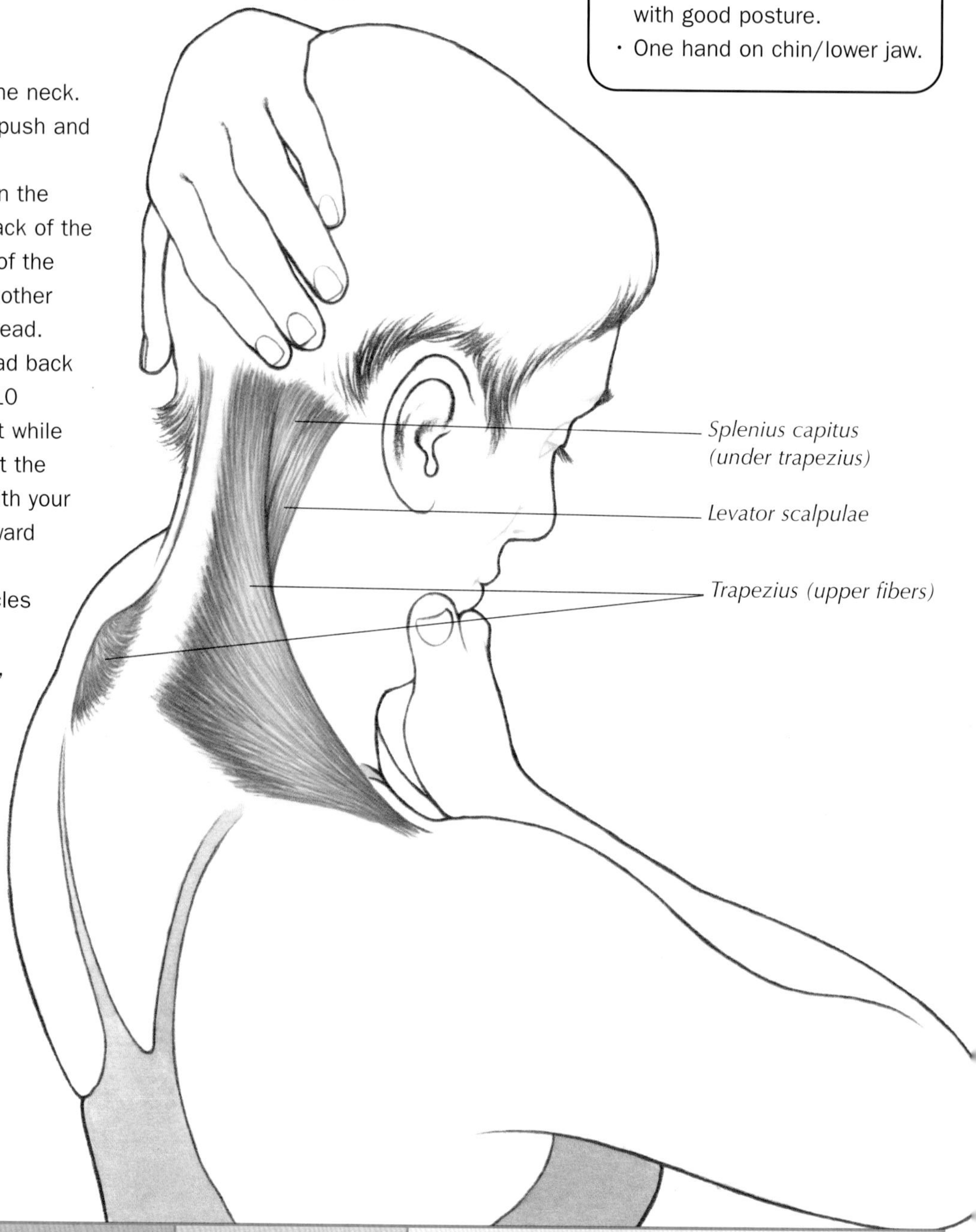

ANALYSIS OF MOVEMENT	JOINTS	JOINT MOVEMENT	MUSCLES STRETCHED
Joint 1	Occipital/atlas C1–C3	Flexion	Trapezius (upper fibers), levator scapula, splenius capitis, splenius cervicis, rectus capitis posterior major and minor, oblique capitis superior, semispinalis capitis

NECK SIDE FLEXORS

Tips for good form:
· Keep the torso upright.
· Keep the head still when you are contracting the muscles.

Basic description:
· Tilt the head and neck away (ear toward shoulder) from the hand holding the bench.
· When you feel a stretch on the side of your neck, inhale, then side-flex the head into the hand with about 10 percent of maximum effort while holding your breath. Resist the movement of your head with your hand so there is no sideways movement of the head.
· After contracting the muscles for five seconds, relax, exhale, and as you do so, move the head farther toward the ear until you find a new position of "bind."
· Repeat three to five times.

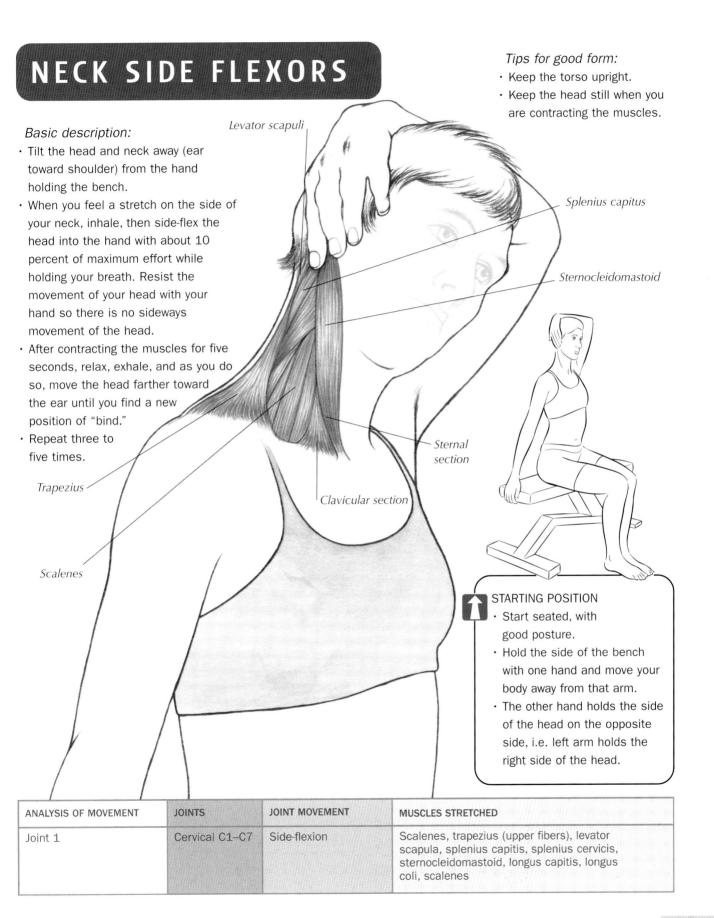

Levator scapuli

Splenius capitus

Sternocleidomastoid

Sternal section

Clavicular section

Trapezius

Scalenes

STARTING POSITION
· Start seated, with good posture.
· Hold the side of the bench with one hand and move your body away from that arm.
· The other hand holds the side of the head on the opposite side, i.e. left arm holds the right side of the head.

ANALYSIS OF MOVEMENT	JOINTS	JOINT MOVEMENT	MUSCLES STRETCHED
Joint 1	Cervical C1–C7	Side-flexion	Scalenes, trapezius (upper fibers), levator scapula, splenius capitis, splenius cervicis, sternocleidomastoid, longus capitis, longus coli, scalenes

PECTORALIS MINOR

Basic description:

· Allow your body weight to drop toward the floor, keeping your shoulders parallel to the ground.
· When you feel a stretch just below your armpit (axilla), inhale and push your elbow and forearm into the ball with about 10 percent of maximum effort while holding your breath.
· After contracting the muscle for five seconds, relax, exhale, and as you do so, move the torso farther toward the floor until you find a new position of "bind."
· Repeat this process three to five times.

Tips for good form:

· Ensure that your shoulder is supported by the ball throughout the stretch.
· When increasing the stretch, allow the scapula (shoulder blade) to move toward the spine.

STARTING POSITION
· Start on all fours. Place one elbow on the apex of a swiss ball.
· Support your shoulder on the ball.

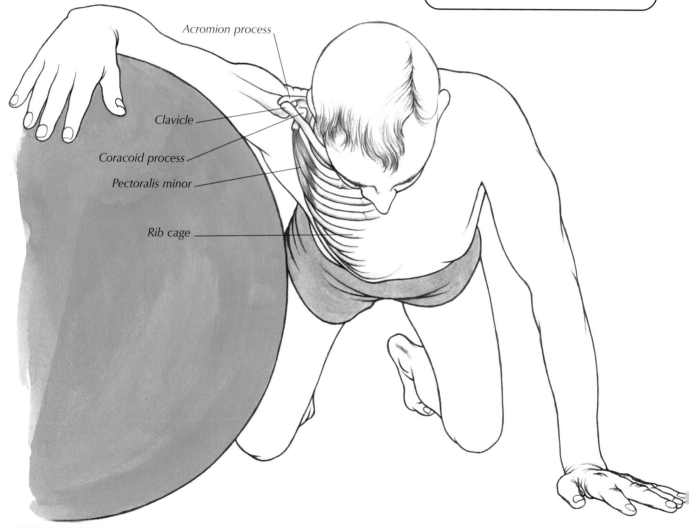

Acromion process

Clavicle

Coracoid process

Pectoralis minor

Rib cage

ANALYSIS OF MOVEMENT	JOINTS	JOINT MOVEMENT	MUSCLES STRETCHED
Joint 1	Scapulothoracic	Retraction	Pectoralis minor

OBLIQUES

Tips for good form:
- Keep your shoulders perpendicular to the ground.

STARTING POSITION
- Lie on your side on a swiss ball. The ball should support the side of your abdomen.
- Place your top leg straight up against a wall. The bottom leg should be bent and slightly in front, helping you to balance.
- Your arms overhead, hold the top wrist with the bottom hand.

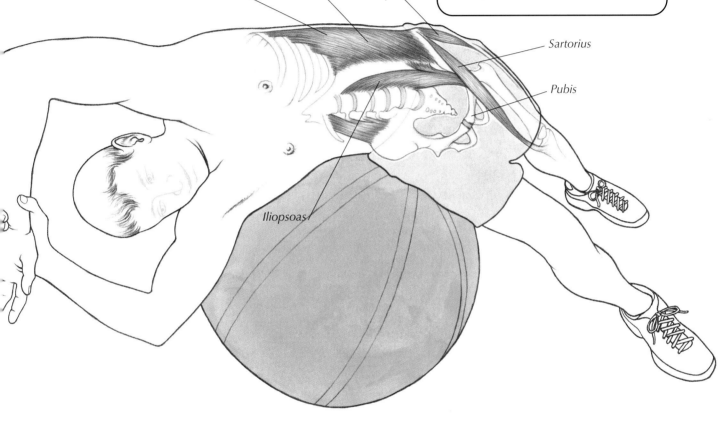

Basic description:
- Side-bend your torso toward the floor, keeping your shoulders perpendicular to the ground.
- When you feel a stretch in the side of your torso, inhale, and attempt to side-crunch upward, but at the same time resist the movement with your bottom hand on your wrist with about 10 percent of maximum effort while holding your breath.
- After contracting the muscle for five seconds, relax, exhale, and as you do so, move the torso farther toward the floor until you find a new position of "bind."
- Repeat this process three to five times.

ANALYSIS OF MOVEMENT	JOINTS	JOINT MOVEMENT	MUSCLES STRETCHED
Joint 1	Thoracic, lumbar spine	Side-flexion	External oblique, internal oblique, quadratus lumborum, iliopsoas
Joint 2	Hip	Adduction	Gluteals, tensor fascia lata, sartorius

ABDOMINALS

Basic description:

- To increase the stretch, extend your knees allowing your head to move farther toward the floor until you feel a stretch in your abdominals.
- Breathe in and out through your nose, allowing your abdomen to rise and fall with each breath. Every two to three breaths, increase the stretch on the exhalation.
- Continue for one to two minutes.

Note: If you ever feel dizzy while looking upward, for instance when looking in overhead cupboards or looking up at airplanes, do not perform this stretch. If you feel faint or dizzy doing this stretch, stop immediately. You may wish to have your neck checked by a trained professional for vertebral artery occlusion.

Tips for good form:
- Ensure the sacrum is in contact with the ball throughout the stretch.

STARTING POSITION
- Begin by lying supine (face up) over a swiss ball, with your sacrum, spine, and head all in contact with the ball, and with knees bent.
- Place your arms overhead.

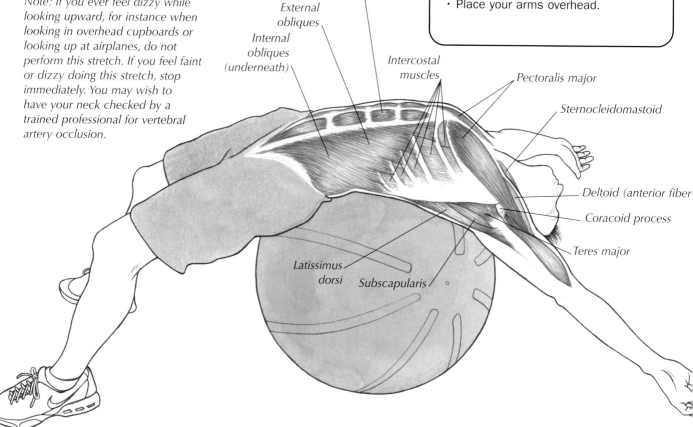

Rectus abdominus
External obliques
Internal obliques (underneath)
Intercostal muscles
Pectoralis major
Sternocleidomastoid
Deltoid (anterior fiber
Coracoid process
Teres major
Latissimus dorsi
Subscapularis

ANALYSIS OF MOVEMENT	JOINTS	JOINT MOVEMENT	MUSCLES STRETCHED
Joint 1	Cervical spine	Extension	Sternocleidomastoid, scalenes (anterior fibers), longus capitis, longus coli
Joint 2	Thoracic and lumbar spine	Extension	Rectus abdominus, external obliques, internal obliques, internal intercostals, serratus posterior inferior
Joint 3	Shoulder	Flexion, abduction, external rotation	Pectoralis major, deltoid (anterior fibers), subscapularis, latissimus dorsi, teres major

LUMBAR ROTATIONS

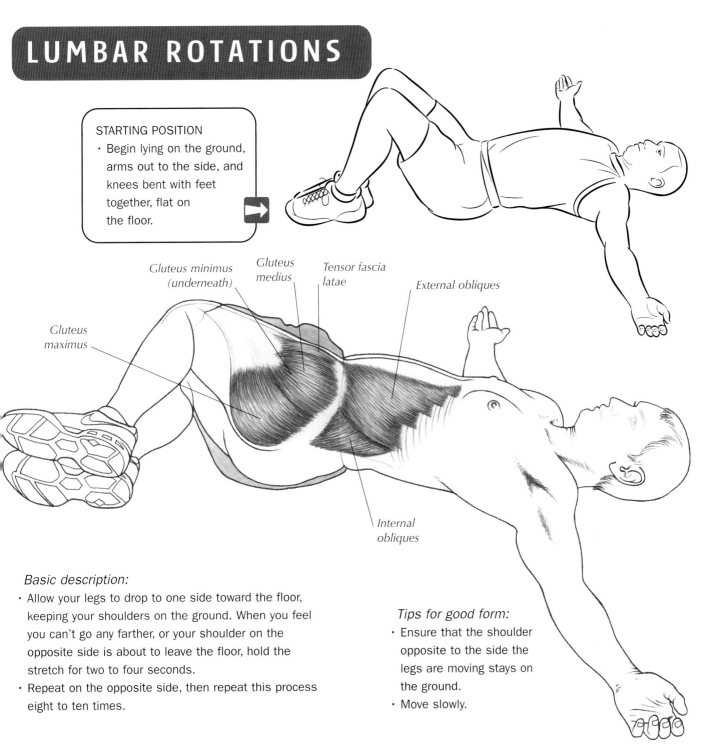

STARTING POSITION
- Begin lying on the ground, arms out to the side, and knees bent with feet together, flat on the floor.

Gluteus maximus

Gluteus minimus (underneath)

Gluteus medius

Tensor fascia latae

External obliques

Internal obliques

Basic description:
- Allow your legs to drop to one side toward the floor, keeping your shoulders on the ground. When you feel you can't go any farther, or your shoulder on the opposite side is about to leave the floor, hold the stretch for two to four seconds.
- Repeat on the opposite side, then repeat this process eight to ten times.

Tips for good form:
- Ensure that the shoulder opposite to the side the legs are moving stays on the ground.
- Move slowly.

ANALYSIS OF MOVEMENT	JOINTS	JOINT MOVEMENT	MUSCLES STRETCHED
Joint 1	Lumbar spine	Rotation	Contralateral: External oblique Ipsilateral: Internal oblique, multifidus, rotatores
Joint 2	Hip	Horizontal abduction	Gluteals, tensor fascia lata, sartorius

TENSOR FASCIA LATA

Basic description:
- Push the pelvis toward the wall while pushing downward on the outer pelvis.
- Breathe slowly and deeply, and relax into the stretch. Hold the stretch for 30–60 seconds, easing into the stretch with every two to three exhalations.

Tips for good form:
- Ensure the pelvis farthest from the wall stays in line with the pelvis nearest to the wall.
- Keep the feet flat on the floor and parallel to the wall.

STARTING POSITION
- Stand side-on to a wall. The leg of the side that is to be stretched is placed across and behind the other leg so it is in adduction and extension.
- Place the forearm closest to the wall against the wall, taking the weight of the torso.
- Place the hand farthest from the wall on the pelvis of the same side.

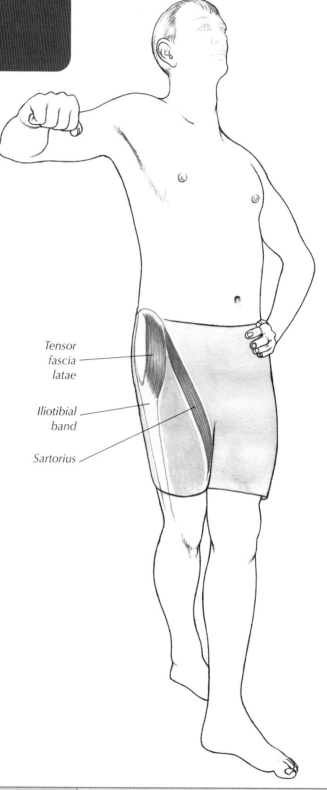

Tensor fascia latae

Iliotibial band

Sartorius

ANALYSIS OF MOVEMENT	JOINTS	JOINT MOVEMENT	MUSCLES STRETCHED
Joint 1	Hip	Adduction, extension	Tensor fascia lata, sartorius

HIP FLEXORS

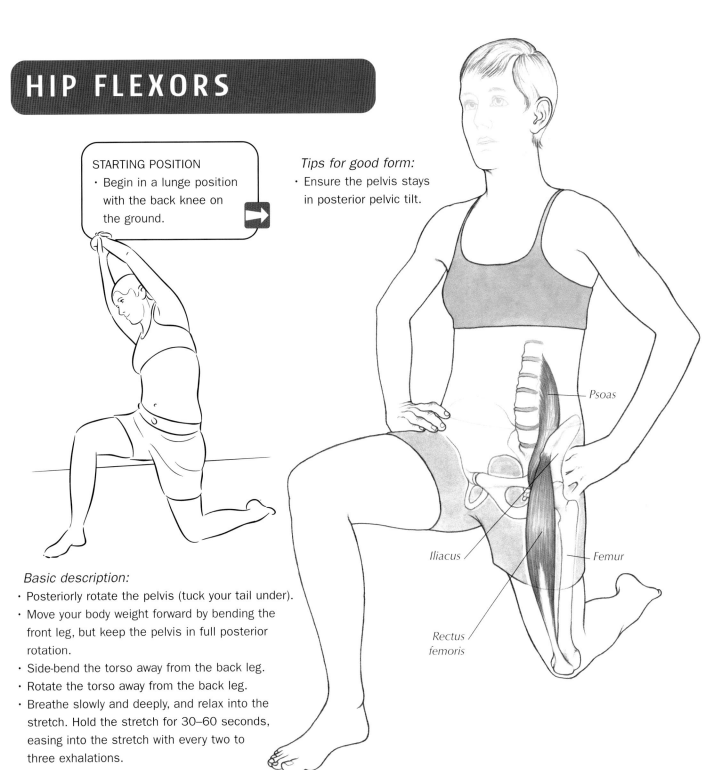

STARTING POSITION
· Begin in a lunge position
  with the back knee on
  the ground.

Tips for good form:
· Ensure the pelvis stays
  in posterior pelvic tilt.

Psoas

Iliacus

Femur

Rectus femoris

Basic description:
· Posteriorly rotate the pelvis (tuck your tail under).
· Move your body weight forward by bending the
  front leg, but keep the pelvis in full posterior
  rotation.
· Side-bend the torso away from the back leg.
· Rotate the torso away from the back leg.
· Breathe slowly and deeply, and relax into the
  stretch. Hold the stretch for 30–60 seconds,
  easing into the stretch with every two to
  three exhalations.

ANALYSIS OF MOVEMENT	JOINTS	JOINT MOVEMENT	MUSCLES STRETCHED
Joint 1	Lumbar spine	Rotation	Contralateral: External oblique Ipsilateral: Internal oblique, multifidus, rotatores
Joint 2	Hip	Horizontal abduction	Gluteals, tensor fascia lata, sartorius

ADDUCTORS

Basic description:
- Increase the bend in the non-stretching leg, moving slightly forward on the ball until you feel a stretch.
- Inhale and contract the foot of the leg that is being stretched into the floor for five seconds.
- Relax and, as you exhale, move farther into the stretch by bending the opposite knee. Hold the new position for five seconds and repeat three to five times.

Tips for good form:
- Keep the knee of the non-stretching leg in line with the second toe.
- Keep the torso upright.
- Keep the whole foot of the leg being stretched in contact with the ground throughout.

STARTING POSITION
- Sit upright on a swiss ball. Take the leg to be stretched out to the side, keep the foot facing forward.
- The other leg should be facing forward at an approximate 45° angle, knees directly in line with the second toe.

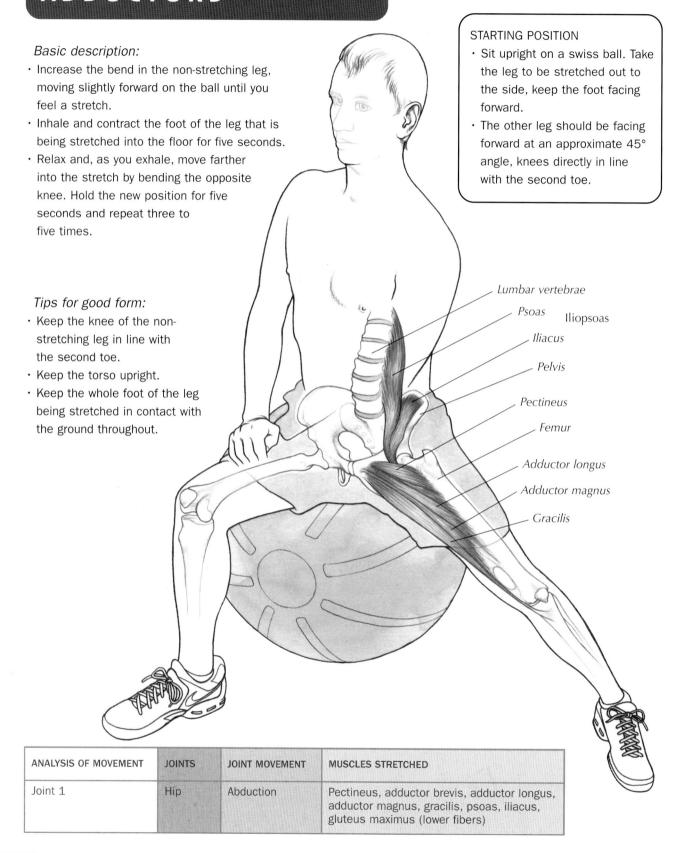

Lumbar vertebrae

Psoas — Iliopsoas

Iliacus

Pelvis

Pectineus

Femur

Adductor longus

Adductor magnus

Gracilis

ANALYSIS OF MOVEMENT	JOINTS	JOINT MOVEMENT	MUSCLES STRETCHED
Joint 1	Hip	Abduction	Pectineus, adductor brevis, adductor longus, adductor magnus, gracilis, psoas, iliacus, gluteus maximus (lower fibers)

HAMSTRINGS—SEATED ON SWISS BALL

Basic description:

- Keeping the skin between your fingers, bend forward from the hips until you feel a stretch in your hamstrings.
- Inhale, then pull your heels into the ground, contracting your hamstrings for five seconds.
- Relax, and as you exhale, lean farther forward from the hips to increase the stretch until you reach a new position of "bind." Hold the new position for five seconds.
- Repeat three to five times or until no more improvement is made.

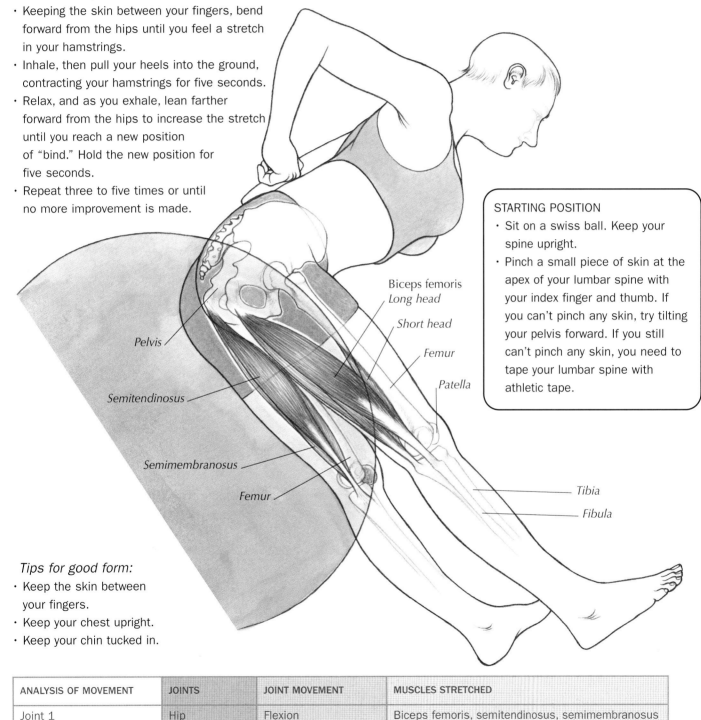

STARTING POSITION
- Sit on a swiss ball. Keep your spine upright.
- Pinch a small piece of skin at the apex of your lumbar spine with your index finger and thumb. If you can't pinch any skin, try tilting your pelvis forward. If you still can't pinch any skin, you need to tape your lumbar spine with athletic tape.

Biceps femoris
Long head

Short head

Femur

Patella

Pelvis

Semitendinosus

Semimembranosus

Femur

Tibia

Fibula

Tips for good form:
- Keep the skin between your fingers.
- Keep your chest upright.
- Keep your chin tucked in.

ANALYSIS OF MOVEMENT	JOINTS	JOINT MOVEMENT	MUSCLES STRETCHED
Joint 1	Hip	Flexion	Biceps femoris, semitendinosus, semimembranosus

CALVES

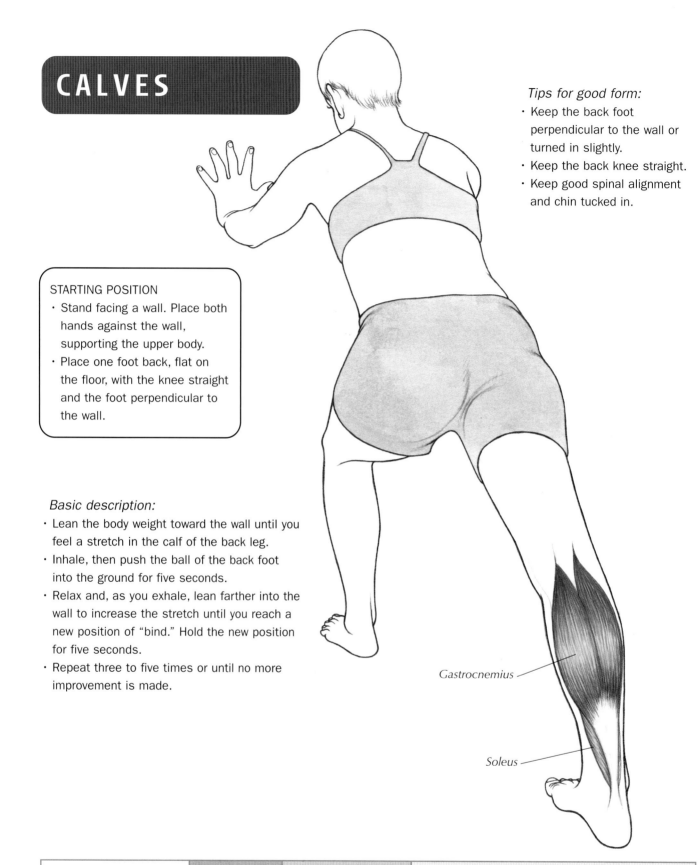

Tips for good form:
- Keep the back foot perpendicular to the wall or turned in slightly.
- Keep the back knee straight.
- Keep good spinal alignment and chin tucked in.

STARTING POSITION
- Stand facing a wall. Place both hands against the wall, supporting the upper body.
- Place one foot back, flat on the floor, with the knee straight and the foot perpendicular to the wall.

Basic description:
- Lean the body weight toward the wall until you feel a stretch in the calf of the back leg.
- Inhale, then push the ball of the back foot into the ground for five seconds.
- Relax and, as you exhale, lean farther into the wall to increase the stretch until you reach a new position of "bind." Hold the new position for five seconds.
- Repeat three to five times or until no more improvement is made.

Gastrocnemius

Soleus

ANALYSIS OF MOVEMENT	JOINTS	JOINT MOVEMENT	MUSCLES STRETCHED
Joint 1	Ankle	Dorsiflexion	Gastrocnemius, soleus, tibialis posterior, peroneus longus and brevis

PRE-EVENT STRETCHING

SQUAT PUSH PRESS

Tips for good form:
- Keep the torso upright, eyes looking straight ahead.
- Keep the knees tracking over the second toes.
- Gently draw the umbilicus toward the spine.

Basic description:
- Inhale, then as you exhale, squat down into a full or partial squat position
- Without pausing at the bottom, return back to the start position while inhaling.
- As you return to the standing position, push the medicine ball overhead.
- As you squat back down, return the ball to the position at the chest.

STARTING POSITION
- Stand upright holding a medicine ball (5–10 percent of body weight) against your chest.

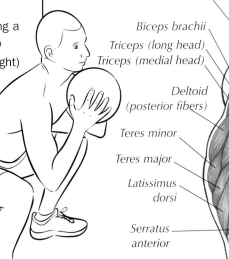

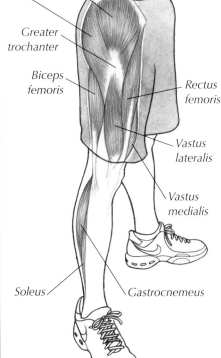

ANALYSIS OF MOVEMENT	JOINTS	JOINT MOVEMENT	MOBILIZING MUSCLES
Joint 1	Elbows	Up: extension Down: flexion	Triceps brachii, anconeus
Joint 2	Shoulder	Up: flexion Down: extension	Deltoid (anterior fibers), pectoralis major (upper fibers), biceps brachii, coracobrachialis
Joint 3	Scapula	Up: upward rotation, abduction Down: downward rotation, adduction	Trapezius (upper and lower fibers), pectoralis minor, serratus anterior
Joint 4	Hip	Up: extension Down: flexion	Gluteus maximus, gluteus medius (posterior fibers), biceps femoris, semitendinosus, semimembranosus, adductor magnus (posterior fibers)
Joint 5	Knee	Up: extension Down: flexion	Vastus medialis, vastus intermedius, vastus lateralis, rectus femoris
Joint 6	Ankle	Up: plantarflexion Down: dorsiflexion	Gastrocnemius, soleus, plantaris, tibialis posterior

STANDING TORSO ROTATIONS

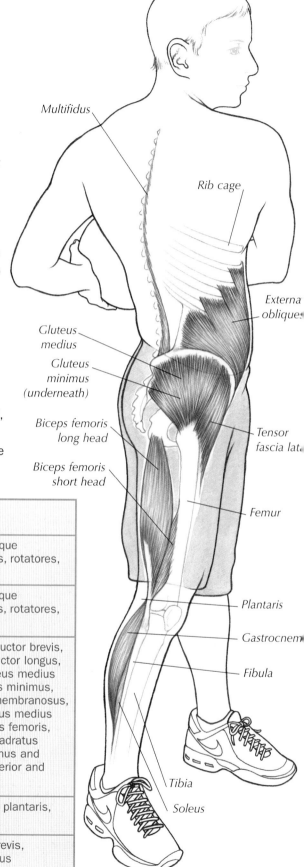

STARTING POSITION
- Stand up straight with a medicine ball just above the navel.
- Feet should be shoulder-width apart.

Tips for good form:
- Keep an upright posture, chest up, and chin tucked in.
- Don't rotate too far or too quickly before you have warmed up sufficiently.

Basic description:
- Rotate the torso gently in each direction.
- As you warm up, you can increase the range of motion and the speed.
- Begin by keeping the feet still. As you warm up, allow the feet to roll inward as you rotate. The head can either stay looking forward, or it can rotate with the spine.
- Complete 10–30 rotations in each direction. Alter the height of the medicine ball to warm up different areas of the back and torso.

ANALYSIS OF MOVEMENT	JOINTS	JOINT MOVEMENT	MOBILIZING MUSCLES
Joint 1	Thoracic spine	Rotation	Ipsilateral: Internal oblique Contralateral: Multifidus, rotatores, external oblique
Joint 2	Lumbar spine	Rotation	Ipsilateral: Internal oblique Contralateral: Multifidus, rotatores, external oblique
Joint 3	Hip	Medial rotation, lateral rotation	Gracilis, pectineus, adductor brevis, adductor magnus, adductor longus, tensor fascia lata, gluteus medius (anterior fibers), gluteus minimus, semitendinosus, semimembranosus, gluteus maximus, gluteus medius (posterior fibers), biceps femoris, sartorius, piriformis, quadratus femoris, obturator internus and externus, gemellus superior and inferior, psoas, iliacus
Joint 4	Ankle	Plantarflexion	Gastrocnemius, soleus, plantaris, tibialis posterior
Joint 5	Metatarsals	Eversion	Peroneus longus and brevis, extensor digitorum longus

Labels on illustration: Multifidus, Rib cage, External obliques, Gluteus medius, Gluteus minimus (underneath), Biceps femoris long head, Biceps femoris short head, Tensor fascia lata, Femur, Plantaris, Gastrocnemius, Fibula, Tibia, Soleus

BEND AND REACH

Tips for good form:
- Keep the torso upright, eyes looking straight ahead.
- Keep the knees tracking over the second toes.
- Gently draw the umbilicus toward the spine.

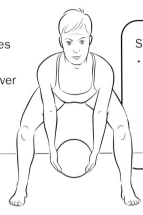

STARTING POSITION
- Stand upright with a medicine ball (5–10 percent of body weight) at arms length in front of your pelvis.

Basic description:
- Inhale, then exhale as you bend forward until the medicine ball goes between your legs while keeping the chest up and eyes looking straight ahead.
- Inhale again as you reach up: the medicine ball goes overhead and you drive your hips forward.
- Without a pause, exhale as you return to the bent forward position with the medicine ball ending up between the legs.
- Complete for 10–20 repetitions, starting slowly, and increasing your speed and range of motion as you warm up.

ANALYSIS OF MOVEMENT	JOINTS	JOINT MOVEMENT	MOBILIZING MUSCLES
Joint 1	Shoulder	Up: flexion Down: extension	Deltoid (anterior fibers), pectoralis major (upper fibers), biceps brachii, coracobrachialis
Joint 2	Scapula	Up: upward rotation, abduction Down: downward rotation, adduction	Trapezius (upper and lower fibers), pectoralis minor, serratus anterior
Joint 3	Thoracic spine	Up: extension Down: flexion to neutral	Spinalis, longissimus, iliocostalis, multifidus, rotatores
Joint 4	Lumbar spine	Up: extension Down: flexion to neutral	Spinalis, longissimus, iliocostalis, multifidus, rotatores, intertransversarii, interspinalis
Joint 5	Hip	Up: extension Down: flexion	Gluteus maximus, gluteus medius (posterior fibers), biceps femoris, semitendinosus, semimembranosus, adductor magnus (posterior fibers)
Joint 6	Knee	Up: extension Down: flexion	Vastus medialis, vastus intermedius, vastus lateralis, rectus femoris
Joint 7	Ankle	Up: Plantarflexion Down: dorsiflexion	Gastrocnemius, soleus, plantaris, tibialis posterior

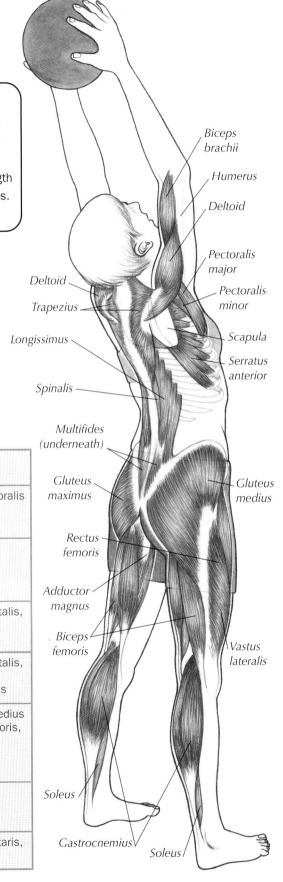

Biceps brachii

Humerus

Deltoid

Pectoralis major

Deltoid

Pectoralis minor

Trapezius

Scapula

Longissimus

Serratus anterior

Spinalis

Multifides (underneath)

Gluteus maximus

Gluteus medius

Rectus femoris

Adductor magnus

Biceps femoris

Vastus lateralis

Soleus

Gastrocnemius

Soleus

WALKING HAMSTRING STRETCH

Tips for good form:
- Keep the spine in a neutral position.
- Don't allow the lumbar spine to flex forward.

Basic description:
- Take one step forward with a straight leg. As you step forward, flex at the hip, but keep the spine straight until you feel a stretch in your hamstrings.
- Step forward with the other leg in the same way.
- Continue to walk like this for 10–20 steps on each leg.

Gluteus medius

Gluteus maximus

Femur

Adductor magnus

Plantaris

Popliteus (underneath)

Gastrocnemius

Soleus

Biceps femoris
Long head
Short head

Semitendinosus

Semimembranosus

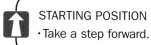

STARTING POSITION
- Take a step forward.

ANALYSIS OF MOVEMENT	JOINTS	JOINT MOVEMENT	MOBILIZING MUSCLES
Joint 1	Hip	Forward leg: flexion Back leg: extension	Gluteus maximus, gluteus medius (posterior fibers), biceps femoris, semitendinosus, semimembranosus, adductor magnus (posterior fibers)
Joint 2	Knee	Extension	Biceps femoris, semitendinosus, semimembranosus, gracilis, sartorius, gastrocnemius, popliteus, plantaris
Joint 3	Ankle	Dorsiflexion	Gastrocnemius, soleus, tibialis posterior

MULTI-DIRECTIONAL LUNGES

Basic description:
· Lunge forward and then back.
· Lunge forward at a 45° angle, keeping
  the torso and feet pointing straight ahead
  and back.
· Lunge to the side, keeping the torso and feet
  pointing straight ahead and back.
· Lunge backward at a 45° angle, keeping
  the torso and feet pointing straight ahead
  and back.
· Lunge backward and back to the start.

STARTING POSITION
· Stand with feet shoulder-
  width apart and torso
  upright, hands on hips.

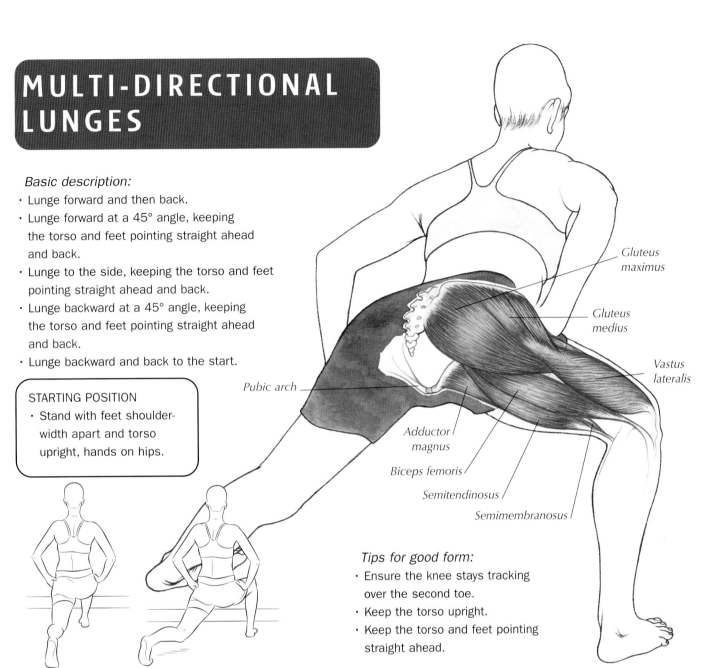

Gluteus maximus
Gluteus medius
Vastus lateralis
Pubic arch
Adductor magnus
Biceps femoris
Semitendinosus
Semimembranosus

Tips for good form:
· Ensure the knee stays tracking
  over the second toe.
· Keep the torso upright.
· Keep the torso and feet pointing
  straight ahead.

ANALYSIS OF MOVEMENT	JOINTS	JOINT MOVEMENT	MOBILIZING MUSCLES
Joint 1	Hip	Flexion, extension, internal, external rotation, adduction, abduction	Gluteus maximus, gluteus medius (posterior fibers), biceps femoris, semitendinosus, semimembranosus, adductor magnus (posterior fibers), tensor fascia lata, sartorius, pectineus, adductor brevis, longus, gracilis, psoas, iliacus, piriformis, quadratus femoris, gemellus superior and inferior, obturator externus and internus
Joint 2	Knee	Extension, medial rotation, lateral rotation	Vastus medialis, vastus intermedius, vastus lateralis, rectus femoris, gracilis, semitendinosus, semimembranosus, sartorius, popliteus, biceps femoris
Joint 3	Ankle	Dorsiflexion, eversion	Tibialis anterior, extensor digitorum longus, extensor hallucis longus, peroneus longus and brevis, extensor digitorum longus

WALKING ARM SWINGS

Tips for good form:
· Keep the torso upright.
· Ensure your arms brush your ears as you swing them past the head.
· Ensure you achieve full ankle plantarflexion as the arms pass directly overhead.

Basic description:
· While walking forward, plantarflex the ankles and swing both arms in a forward direction in a circle for 10–20 arm swings
· Then complete a further 10–20 arm swings in a backward direction while continuing to walk forward and plantarflex the ankles.
· Start slowly and increase the speed of movement as you warm up.

STARTING POSITION
· Stand with feet shoulder-width apart and torso upright, hands by your sides.

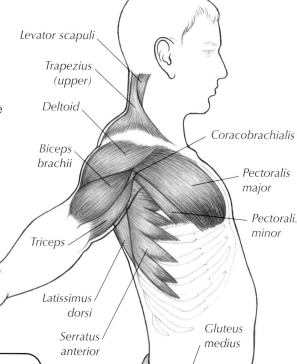

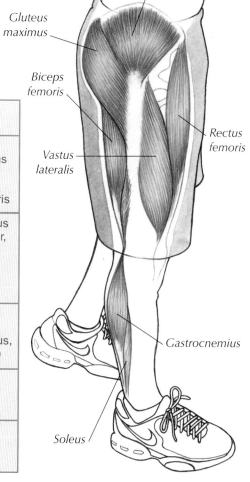

ANALYSIS OF MOVEMENT	JOINTS	JOINT MOVEMENT	MOBILIZING MUSCLES
Joint 1	Shoulder	Circumduction	Deltoid, pectoralis major, biceps brachii, coracobrachialis, latissimus dorsi, teres major, infraspinatus, teres minor, triceps brachii (long head), supraspinatus, subscapularis
Joint 2	Scapula	Upward rotation, abduction, downward rotation, adduction, elevation, depression	Trapezius, pectoralis minor, serratus anterior, rhomboid major and minor, levator scapula
Joint 3	Hip	Back leg: extension, Forward leg: flexion	Gluteus maximus, gluteus medius (posterior fibers), biceps femoris, semitendinosus, semimembranosus, adductor magnus (posterior fibers)
Joint 4	Knee	Up: extension Down: flexion	Vastus medialis, vastus intermedius, vastus lateralis, rectus femoris
Joint 5	Ankle	Up: plantarflexion Down: dorsiflexion	Gastrocnemius, soleus, tibialis posterior

Labels on figure: Levator scapuli, Trapezius (upper), Deltoid, Coracobrachialis, Biceps brachii, Pectoralis major, Pectoralis minor, Triceps, Latissimus dorsi, Serratus anterior, Gluteus medius, Gluteus maximus, Biceps femoris, Rectus femoris, Vastus lateralis, Gastrocnemius, Soleus

SIDE SHUFFLE

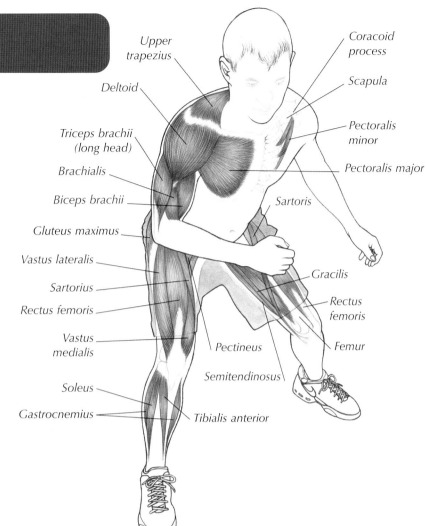

Basic description:
- Side shuffle with quick feet for a yard or so at a 45° angle.
- Change direction quickly at a 90° angle and side shuffle for another yard or so.
- Continue for several yards.

Tips for good form:
- Keep on the balls of your feet with knees bent.
- Drive off the back leg and do not cross over the legs.
- Keep your torso and head up and look in the direction you are moving.
- Drive the arms with each leg movement.

STARTING POSITION
- Begin on the balls of your feet, hips slightly lowered by bending your knees.

Image labels: Upper trapezius, Deltoid, Triceps brachii (long head), Brachialis, Biceps brachii, Gluteus maximus, Vastus lateralis, Sartorius, Rectus femoris, Vastus medialis, Soleus, Gastrocnemius, Coracoid process, Scapula, Pectoralis minor, Pectoralis major, Sartoris, Gracilis, Rectus femoris, Femur, Pectineus, Semitendinosus, Tibialis anterior

ANALYSIS OF MOVEMENT	JOINTS	JOINT MOVEMENT	MOBILIZING MUSCLES
Joint 1	Shoulder	Flexion, extension	Deltoid (anterior fibers), pectoralis major (upper fibers), biceps brachii, Deltoid (posterior fibers), latissimus dorsi, teres major, infraspinatus, teres minor, pectoralis major (lower fibers), triceps brachii (long head)
Joint 2	Scapula	Upward rotation, abduction, downward rotation, adduction	Trapezius, pectoralis minor, serratus anterior, rhomboid major and minor, levator scapula
Joint 3	Hip	Abduction, adduction, medial rotation, lateral rotation	Gluteus maximus, gluteus medius, gluteus minimus, tensor fascia lata, sartorius, pectineus, adductor brevis, longus and magnus, psoas major, iliacus, gracilis, semitendinosus, semimembranosus, piriformis, quadratus femoris, gemellus superior and inferior, obturator externus and internus
Joint 4	Knee	Flexion, extension	Biceps femoris, semitendinosus, semimembranosus, gracilis, sartorius, gastrocnemius, popliteus, plantaris vastus medialis, vastus intermedius, vastus lateralis, rectus femoris
Joint 5	Ankle	Plantarflexion, dorsiflexion,	Gastrocnemius, soleus, tibialis posterior, Tibialis anterior, extensor digitorum longus, extensor hallucis longus
Joint 6	Foot	Inversion, eversion	Tibialis anterior and posterior, flexor digitorum longus, flexor hallucis longus, extensor hallucis longus, peroneus longus and brevis, extensor digitorum longus

KNEE-UPS

Basic description:
· Jog at a moderate speed, lifting the knees up in front of you until your knee hits your hand.
· Continue for 10–30 yards.

STARTING POSITION
· Stand with feet shoulder-width apart and torso upright, hands held in front of you at hip level.

Tips for good form:
· Keep the torso upright.
· Keep the foot contact with the ground as short as possible.

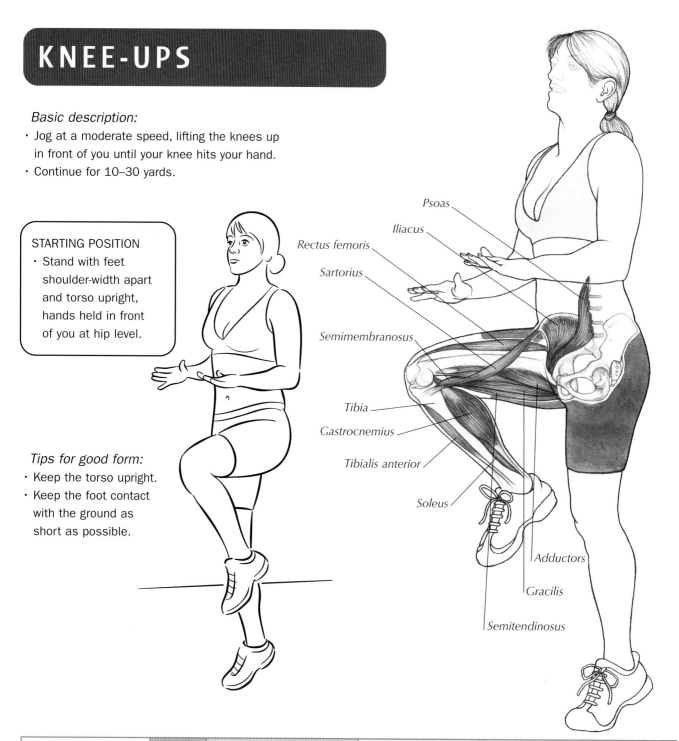

Psoas
Iliacus
Rectus femoris
Sartorius
Semimembranosus
Tibia
Gastrocnemius
Tibialis anterior
Soleus
Adductors
Gracilis
Semitendinosus

ANALYSIS OF MOVEMENT	JOINTS	JOINT MOVEMENT	MOBILIZING MUSCLES
Joint 1	Hip	Flexion, extension	Psoas, iliacus, rectus femoris, tensor fascia lata, sartorius, adductor brevis, longus and magnus, gluteus medius (anterior and posterior fibers), gluteus minimus
Joint 2	Knee	Flexion, extension	Biceps femoris, semitendinosus, semimembranosus, gracilis, sartorius, gastrocnemius, popliteus, plantaris
Joint 3	Ankle	Plantarflexion, dorsiflexion	Gastrocnemius, soleus, tibialis posterior, tibialis anterior, extensor digitorum longus, extensor hallucis longus

HEEL KICKS

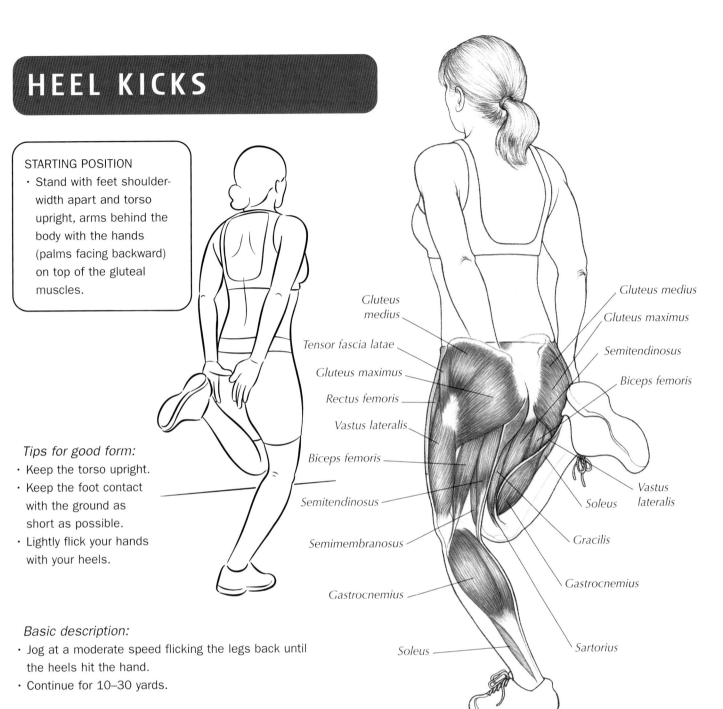

STARTING POSITION
- Stand with feet shoulder-width apart and torso upright, arms behind the body with the hands (palms facing backward) on top of the gluteal muscles.

Tips for good form:
- Keep the torso upright.
- Keep the foot contact with the ground as short as possible.
- Lightly flick your hands with your heels.

Basic description:
- Jog at a moderate speed flicking the legs back until the heels hit the hand.
- Continue for 10–30 yards.

Gluteus medius

Tensor fascia latae

Gluteus maximus

Rectus femoris

Vastus lateralis

Biceps femoris

Semitendinosus

Semimembranosus

Gastrocnemius

Soleus

Gluteus medius

Gluteus maximus

Semitendinosus

Biceps femoris

Vastus lateralis

Soleus

Gracilis

Gastrocnemius

Sartorius

ANALYSIS OF MOVEMENT	JOINTS	JOINT MOVEMENT	MOBILIZING MUSCLES
Joint 1	Hip	Flexion, extension	Psoas, iliacus, rectus femoris, tensor fascia lata, sartorius, adductor brevis, longus and magnus, gluteus medius (anterior and posterior fibers), gluteus minimus, gluteus maximus, biceps femoris, semitendinosus, semimembranosus
Joint 2	Knee	Flexion, extension	Biceps femoris, semitendinosus, semimembranosus, gracilis, sartorius, gastrocnemius, popliteus, plantaris, vastus medialis, vastus intermedius, vastus lateralis, rectus femoris
Joint 3	Ankle	Plantarflexion, dorsiflexion	Gastrocnemius, soleus, tibialis posterior, tibialis anterior, extensor digitorum longus, extensor hallucis longus

"The core" is a real buzz word these days in the fields of health and performance. However, many talk about the core believing they are just talking about the abdominal musculature and perhaps the lower back, which is not the case.

The core is made up of an "inner'"and an "outer" unit. The muscles of the outer unit are discussed on pages 53–54. The muscles of the inner unit of the core are the multifidus, pelvic floor, transversus abdominus, and the diaphragm. These muscles create a cylinder-like, or corset-like, structure around the lumbar spine from the base of the ribs down to the pelvis. These muscles all work together to help stabilize the lumbar spine, the pelvis, and the rib cage. They do this through three known mechanisms: increasing intra-abdominal pressure, thoraco-lumbar fascia gain, and the hydraulic amplifier mechanism. It is beyond the scope of this book to explain these mechanisms, but the references on page 134 may provide more detailed information.

Stability of the spine, pelvis, and rib cage are crucial to prevent injury, and to provide a foundation for the limbs to create movement efficiently, powerfully, and safely. The more stability created by the inner unit, the more power can be produced through the limbs, and the likelihood of injury is reduced.

All movement emanates from the core outward. This means that the inner unit muscles of the core contract prior to the more superficial phasic muscles. Or to put it another way, the inner unit muscles contract to stabilize the lumbar spine, pelvis, and rib cage prior to muscles of the outer unit. For instance, the transversus abdominus, pelvic floor, and diaphragm have been shown to contract on average 30 milliseconds prior to an arm movement and 110 milliseconds prior to a leg movement in all directions of limb movement (C. Richardson, G. Jull, P. Hodges, and J. Hides, *Therapeutic Exercise for Spinal Segmental Stabilization in Low Back Pain*). The outer unit muscles of the trunk contract later than the inner unit muscles, and often contract later than the movement of the limb itself. The timing of contraction of outer unit trunk muscles is dependent on the direction of movement of the limb. The difference between the inner unit muscles of the core is that they are controlled by the central nervous system independently of the outer unit trunk muscles. It has also been shown that when one muscle of the inner unit contracts, the other muscles of the inner unit also contract. This suggests that these muscles are on the same neurological reflexive loop.

The muscles of the inner unit of the core have been shown to be inhibited due to pain or reflex inhibition (C. Richardson, G. Jull, P. Hodges, and J. Hides, *Therapeutic Exercise for Spinal Segmental Stabilization in Low Back Pain*), sensory-motor amnesia (T. Hannah, *Somatics*), and visero-somato reflex (R. Gerwin, *Myofascial and Visceral Pain Syndromes: Visceral-Somatic Pain Representations*). In simple terms, pain in the abdominal region or lumbar spine, a lack of physical activity, or inflammation of an internal organ can cause these inner unit muscles to be inhibited and unable to contract normally. This leaves the spine exposed, increases the likelihood of injury, and reduces the amount of power available.

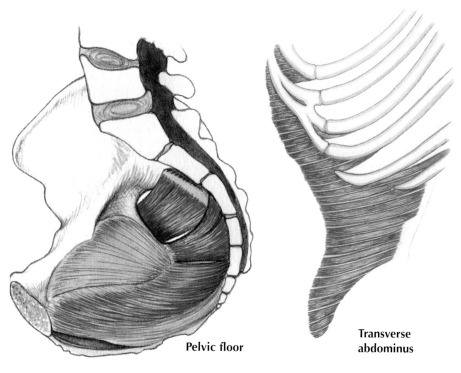

Pelvic floor

Transverse abdominus

This concept is important to understand when training in the gym. There are many different views among experts with regard to training the inner unit. Some suggest not consciously focusing on it at all ,and instead just stiffening all the abdominal muscles, known as "bracing," to stabilize the spine. This technique does have its place and does help to increase stability in healthy individuals. However, in instances where the inner unit

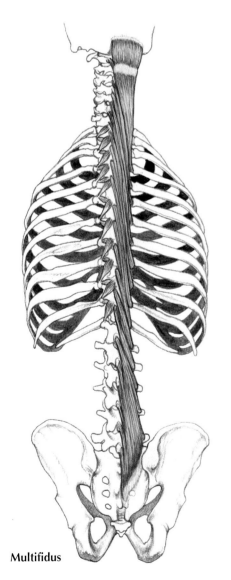

Multifidus

muscles may be inhibited, bracing may not be effective because it is the inner unit muscles that provide segmental stability of the vertebral bodies. An inability to stabilize an individual spinal segment during a heavy lift could expose the spine to uncontrolled shear or torsion (see glossary, page 135), and result in serious injury. In addition, the bracing technique can also limit rotation of the torso, an action used in most movements in sport. Bracing while rotating the torso is analogous to driving your car with the emergency brake on! You will waste a lot of energy and limit the amount of rotation possible.

What I have found to work in my clinical practice is a technique taught to me by Paul Chek, the founder of the C.H.E.K (Corrective Holistic Exercise Kinesiology) Institute. The technique involves initially using a conscious focus on inner unit contraction in an isolated environment when someone has a dysfunctional inner unit (see the four-point tummy vacuum on page 50). I would estimate that around 90 percent of athletes I work with have a dysfunctional inner unit when I first assess them. The four-point tummy vacuum allows the athlete to contract these muscles consciously without having to think about other muscle movements. As the athlete becomes more confident with the muscular contraction, the exercises can be progressed to include co-ordination with outer unit muscles (see the horse stance exercises on pages 51 and 52). The horse stance position is particularly effective, as the viscera create a stretch and

excite the muscle spindles (see glossary, page 135) of the transversus abdominus muscle, which increases its ability to contract. In addition, the horse stance position, when performed correctly, creates a neutral spine position, from which more muscle fibers of the transversus abdominus are able to contract (C. Richardson, G. Jull, P. Hodges, and J. Hides, *Therapeutic Exercise for Spinal Segmental Stabilization in Low Back Pain*).

Ultimately, you will be required to integrate contraction of the inner unit muscles with your outer unit muscles subconsciously. It has been indicated that it takes 300 repetitions to create a new motor program (R. Schmidt, *Motor Learning, and Performance*) or 3,000 to 5,500 repetitions to over-write an existing motor program (P. Chek, *Movement That Matters*). Therefore, it will take you somewhere between 300 and 5,500 repetitions to make this contraction automatic.

It is advised that you complete inner unit exercises at the end of gym workouts to ensure you do not fatigue the stabilizer muscles prior to completing large compound movements (see glossary, page 135).

FOUR-POINT TUMMY VACUUM

Basic description:
· Inhale, allowing the abdomen to drop down toward the ground.
· As you exhale, gently draw the umbilicus (belly button) toward the spine, or imagine using the toilet and having to stop the flow (this activates your pelvic floor muscles), without any movement in the spine.
· Hold the contraction for ten seconds.
· Inhale again and repeat for ten repetitions.

STARTING POSITION
· Position yourself on all fours (horse stance position).
· Your hands should be directly under the shoulders, with knees directly under the hips.
· A stick or dowel rod can be placed on the spine to help create a "neutral" spine. The gap between the stick and the lumbar spine should be equal to the width of your hand.

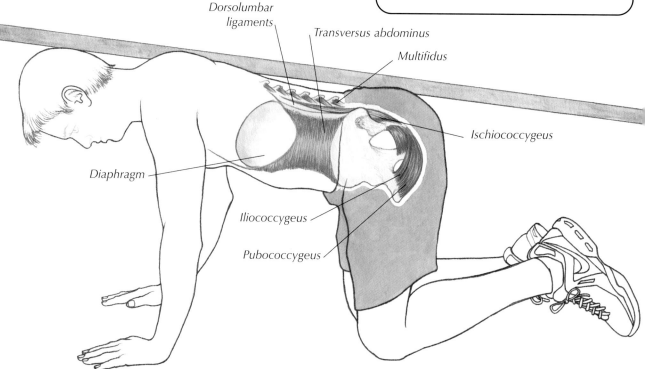

Dorsolumbar ligaments

Transversus abdominus

Multifidus

Ischiococcygeus

Diaphragm

Iliococcygeus

Pubococcygeus

Tips for good form:
· Keep the spine in a neutral position.
· Ensure that as you breathe in, the abdomen drops toward the ground.

ANALYSIS OF MOVEMENT	JOINTS	JOINT MOVEMENT	STABILIZING MUSCLES
Joint 1	Rib cage	Stabilization	Diaphragm, transversus abdominus
Joint 2	Lumbar spine	Stabilization	Transversus abdominus, multifidus
Joint 3	Pelvis	Stabilization	Transversus abdominus, puborectalis, pubococcygeus, iliococcygeus, ischiococcygeus

HORSE STANCE VERTICAL

Basic description:
- Inhale, allowing the abdomen to drop down toward the ground.
- As you exhale, gently draw the umbilicus (belly button) toward the spine, or imagine using the toilet and having to stop the flow (this activates your pelvic floor muscles), without any movement in the spine.
- Simultaneously, raise one hand and the opposite knee a fraction of an inch off the floor. Keep the spine in neutral, and try to avoid any twisting of the spine or any side-to-side movement of the torso or hips.
- Hold the contraction for five to ten seconds, then change sides for five to ten seconds.
- Breathe naturally while maintaining the umbilicus, drawing in, and repeating 10 times on each side.

STARTING POSITION
- Position yourself on all fours (horse stance position).
- Your hands should be directly under the shoulders, with knees directly under the hips.
- A stick or dowel rod can be placed on the spine to help create a "neutral" spine. The gap between the stick and the lumbar spine should be equal to the width of your hand.

Tips for good form:
- Keep the spine in a neutral position.
- Keep your umbilicus drawn in throughout the whole set.

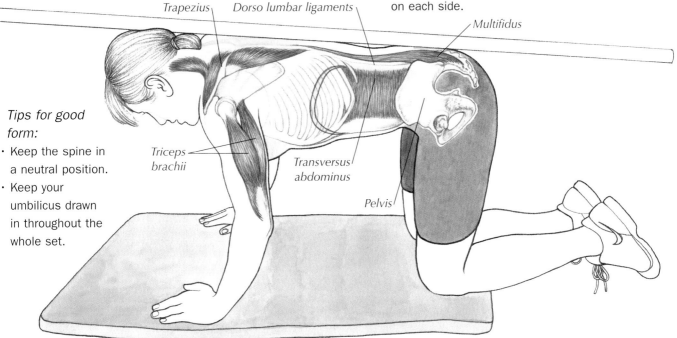

Trapezius | Dorso lumbar ligaments | Multifidus
Triceps brachii | Transversus abdominus | Pelvis

ANALYSIS OF MOVEMENT	JOINTS	JOINT MOVEMENT	MOBILIZING MUSCLES
Joint 1	Rib cage	Stabilization	Diaphragm, transversus abdominus
Joint 2	Lumbar spine	Stabilization Rotation	Transversus abdominus, multifidus External and internal obliques, rotatores
Joint 3	Pelvis	Stabilization	Transversus abdominus, puborectalis, pubococcygeus, iliococcygeus, ischiococcygeus
Joint 4	Scapula	Adduction	Trapezius (middle fibers), rhomboid major and minor (lifted side)
Joint 5	Elbow	Stabilization	Triceps brachii (grounded side)

HORSE STANCE HORIZONTAL

STARTING POSITION
- Position yourself on all fours (horse stance position).
- Your hands should be directly under the shoulders, with knees directly under the hips.
- A stick or dowel rod can be placed on the spine to help create a "neutral" spine. The gap between the stick and the lumbar spine should be equal to the width of your hand.

Basic description:
- Inhale, allowing the abdomen to drop down toward the ground.
- As you exhale, gently draw the umbilicus (belly button) toward the spine, or imagine using the toilet and having to stop the flow (this activates your pelvic floor muscles), without any movement in the spine.
- Then, simultaneously raise one arm and the opposite leg out until parallel to the ground, with the arm at a 45° angle to the torso. Keep the spine in neutral and try to avoid any twisting of the spine, or any side-to-side movement of the torso or hips.
- Hold the contraction for five to ten seconds, then change sides.
- Breathe naturally while maintaining the umbilicus, drawing in and repeating 10 times on each side.

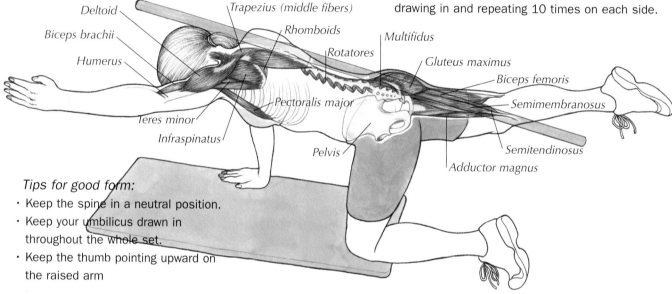

Deltoid, Biceps brachii, Humerus, Trapezius (middle fibers), Rhomboids, Rotatores, Multifidus, Gluteus maximus, Biceps femoris, Pectoralis major, Semimembranosus, Teres minor, Infraspinatus, Pelvis, Semitendinosus, Adductor magnus

Tips for good form:
- Keep the spine in a neutral position.
- Keep your umbilicus drawn in throughout the whole set.
- Keep the thumb pointing upward on the raised arm

ANALYSIS OF MOVEMENT	JOINTS	JOINT MOVEMENT	MOBILIZING MUSCLES
Joint 1	Rib cage	Stabilization	Diaphragm, transversus abdominus
Joint 2	Lumbar spine	Stabilization Rotation	Transversus abdominus, multifidus External and internal obliques, rotatores
Joint 3	Pelvis	Stabilization	Transversus abdominus, puborectalis, pubococcygeus, iliococcygeus, ischiococcygeus
Joint 4	Scapula	Adduction	Trapezius (middle fibers), rhomboid major and minor (lifted side)
Joint 5	Elbow	Stabilization	Triceps brachii (grounded side)
Joint 6	Shoulder	Flexion, abduction external rotation	Deltoid, pectoralis major (upper fibers), biceps brachii, supraspinatus, infraspinatus, teres minor
Joint 7	Hip	Extension	Gluteus maximus, gluteus medius (posterior fibers), biceps femoris, semitendinosus, semimembranosus, adductor magnus (posterior fibers)

The "outer unit" of the core is made up of four distinct systems: the anterior oblique, posterior oblique, lateral, and deep longitudinal systems. The outer unit has a dual role: it helps the inner unit to stabilize, and is also required to generate movement. Whereas the inner unit muscles are tonic in nature (stabilizers), the outer unit muscles are generally phasic (mobilizers).

The anterior oblique system comprises the external obliques working in conjunction with the internal oblique and adductor group on the opposite side. They work in conjunction with each other to create rotation in the torso and pelvis. The system helps to stabilize the torso above the stance leg in gait, and allows for optimal positioning of the heel for heel strike.

In addition to gait, the anterior oblique system plays a significant role in many sporting movements such as throwing a ball, serving in tennis, driving a golf ball, and kicking in martial arts and soccer. The anterior oblique system can be trained using the "push" and "twist" patterns in this book (see pages 72–78).

The posterior oblique system consists of the gluteus maximus and latissimus dorsi on the opposite side, and the thoracolumbar fascia that connects them. The posterior oblique system works during gait to propel the body forward during the propulsive phase of gait as the gluteus maximus and contralateral latissimus dorsi contract simultaneously, creating extension at the hip and shoulder joints.

The posterior oblique system also serves to stabilize the sacroiliac joint of the stance leg during gait. This is

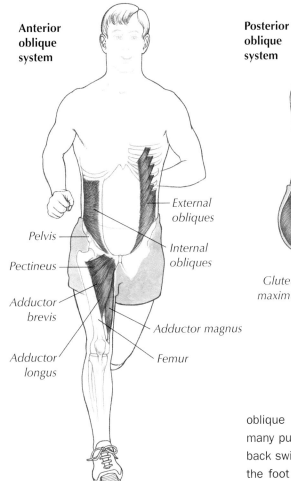

Anterior oblique system

- External obliques
- Pelvis
- Internal obliques
- Pectineus
- Adductor brevis
- Adductor magnus
- Adductor longus
- Femur

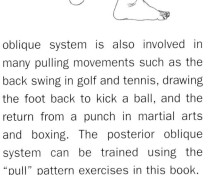

Posterior oblique system

- Scapula
- Latissimus dorsi
- Gluteus maximus

due to fibers of the gluteus maximus and thoracolumbar fascia, which then blend into the contralateral latissimus dorsi and run perpendicular to the sacroiliac joint. When the muscles simultaneously contract, they compress the joint, creating what is known as "force closure" (see glossary, page 135) of the sacroiliac joint. The system also stores kinetic energy in the thoracolumbar fascia as the muscles simultaneously contract. This energy is then released as the muscles relax, which reduces the energy requirement for gait, therefore improving efficiency.

In addition to gait, the posterior

oblique system is also involved in many pulling movements such as the back swing in golf and tennis, drawing the foot back to kick a ball, and the return from a punch in martial arts and boxing. The posterior oblique system can be trained using the "pull" pattern exercises in this book.

The lateral system consists of the adductor group, the same side (Ipsilateral) gluteus medius and minimus, and the opposite side (contralateral) quadratus lumborum. The lateral system works during gait to stabilize the torso above the stance leg. It does this by an equal contraction of the gluteals and adductors to create stability at the hip joint. The quadratus lumborum works to raise or "hike" the hip to allow enough space for the swinging leg during gait.

The lateral system is crucial for any sport that involves gait. My own experience has shown me that the gluteus medius muscle is often weak, especially in females, which increases the likelihood of injury to the ankle, knee, hip, and lower back. It will also reduce efficiency, power, and speed during running. The lateral system can be developed using the "lunge" patterns in this book.

The deep longitudinal system consists of the peroneus longus, biceps femoris, sacrotuberous ligament, thoracolumbar fascia, and erector spinae group. During the late swing phase of gait, the pelvis is posteriorly rotated, helping to create stability through the sacroiliac joint prior to heel strike through form closure (also known as passive closure)—see glossary, page 135. In addition, the biceps femoris contracts to slow down hip flexion and knee extension. It is suggested that 18 percent of the tension created by the biceps femoris is transferred to the peroneus longus, which works in conjunction with the tibialis anterior to stabilize the foot and ankle at heel strike. The hamstrings also create tension through the sacrotuberous ligament, which helps to stabilize the sacroiliac joint of the stance leg through force close (active closure). The tension from the sacrotuberous ligament transfers into the thoracolumbar fascia and erector spinae muscle group. The kinetic energy is then transmitted into the torso, aiding rotation of the spine, and reducing the energy cost of gait.

During running, a ground reaction force of five to seven times body weight is created. Therefore, a 200 lb (90 kg) man would create 1,000–1,400 lbs (450–630 kg) of force that needs to be dissipated prior to reaching the skull. The force transfers from the ground through the muscles of the deep longitudinal system, and is dissipated through the para-spinal muscles, which aids the rotation of the spine.

In instances where the transversus abdominus is inhibited, it has been theorized that the biceps femoris will contract harder to put tension through the sacrotuberous ligament to create adequate force closure in the sacroiliac joint. It is also theorized that this may lead to an increased incidence of biceps femoris strains in sprinters (P. Chek, *Back Strong & Beltless—Part 3*).

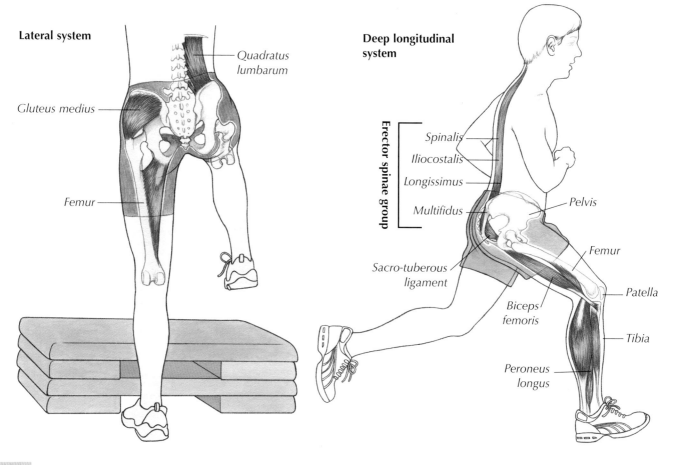

Lateral system

Quadratus lumbarum

Gluteus medius

Femur

Deep longitudinal system

Erector spinae group

Spinalis
Iliocostalis
Longissimus
Multifidus

Sacro-tuberous ligament

Biceps femoris

Peroneus longus

Pelvis

Femur

Patella

Tibia

In the book *Movement that Matters,* Paul Chek suggests that "the selective pressures of evolution must have resulted in human anatomy that was specifically designed to meet the demands of nature."

He also goes on to say that "if developmental man could not twist, pull, lunge, bend, squat, and push from the standing position or could not effectively ambulate, then chances of survival would dwindle severely."

Therefore, he proposed that there are seven Primal Pattern® Movements:

- Lunge
- Squat
- Bend
- Push
- Pull
- Twist
- Gait

This means that if an athlete is unable to perform all the required Primal Pattern® Movements in their sport, their performance will be reduced, and the likelihood of injury will be increased.

All movements in sport can be broken down into Primal Pattern® Movements, or a combination of these. For example, when throwing a ball the movement begins with a lunge, then a twist, then finally a push with extension of the elbow and flexion of the wrist. A jump shot in basketball is a squat, followed by a push. A drive in golf is a bend, combined with a twist.

Schmidt suggested in *Motor Learning and Performance* that the brain stores movement patterns, known as generalized motor programs, and not the individual control of each muscle. Therefore, the brain has a

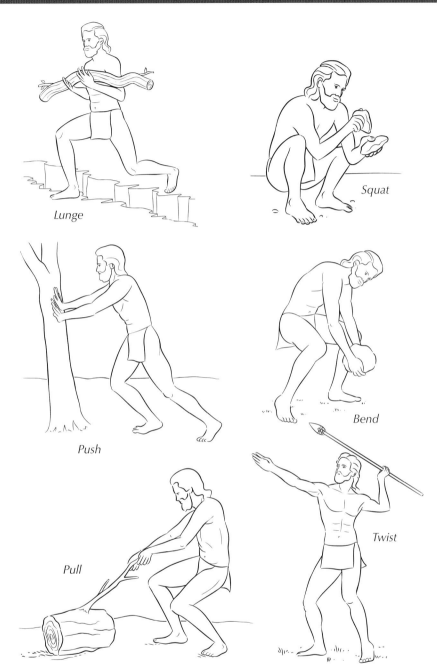

Lunge

Squat

Push

Bend

Pull

Twist

"kick the ball" motor program and not a "stabilize the torso, extend the hip, flex the shoulder, then rotate the torso with flexion of the hip, and extension of the shoulder" motor program. Hence the saying, "train the movement, not the muscles." Schmidt recognized that motor programs can be used to train groups of movements with a similar

timing. For instance, the squat pattern can be used to train for jumping, as the timing of the movement at the ankle, knee, and hip is the same.

In terms of conditioning for sport, we can highlight the required Primal Pattern® Movements for any particular sport, and begin to train those independently until perfect technique is achieved, including integration with the inner unit of the core. Once perfection or near-perfection has been established, a combination of movement patterns can be trained that are relevant to the sport.

It should also be noted that training the actual sporting movement with a heavy load can be detrimental to the motor program involved with a particular sport. For instance, as a tennis player you probably wouldn't want to train with a dumb-bell or cable machine, replicating your ground stokes. This could adversely affect your technique and the timing of your ground strokes. However, you *can* condition your twist, lunge, push, pull, bend, and squat, which you will require during a game of tennis. As Schmidt has suggested, as long as the relative timing is similar, you will get a "carry-over" effect in sporting performance.

In the following sections, I have listed each Primal Pattern® Movement with a beginner, intermediate, and advanced level exercise for each one. You must analyze your particular sport and highlight which Primal Pattern® Movements are required in it. If you have little time for workouts, you'll need to prioritize the Primal Pattern® Movements most vital to your sport, and focus on conditioning in those patterns.

The exercises shown are not an exhaustive list and may not be appropriate for all sports. You need to consider whether you need to condition the pattern on one leg, two legs or both, and whether your sporting environment is on a stable or unpredictable surface (see page 130). By analyzing your sport, you may need to use some creativity to find the best ways to condition each pattern to optimize your performance.

Please note that just because you may be able to do one Primal Pattern® Movement perfectly, it doesn't mean that you will be able to do them all perfectly. Ensure that you are able to perform each movement with good form (check the "tips for good form" relevant to each exercise). Once you can perform the beginner exercise perfectly, move on to the intermediate level. If appropriate to your particular sport, move to the advanced level once you have perfected the intermediate level exercise.

When we are learning movement patterns, slow speeds need to be used. Once good skill of movement has been achieved, the speed of movement can be increased gradually.

GAIT

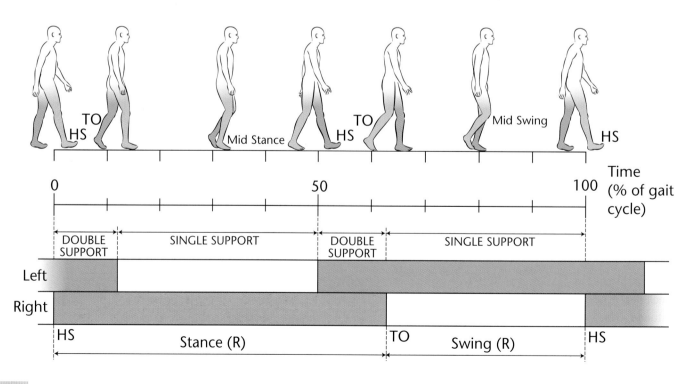

Gait is a word that describes how animals ambulate on their limbs. We humans tend to ambulate most of the time on two legs, particularly during most sports. Until farming techniques were developed over the last 10,000 years in Asia and 3,000 years in Europe, human gait was essential for hunting to enable us to survive. Prior to farming, most tribes would have been nomadic, and would have followed the animal herds for many miles to keep a source of high-energy foods available. When hunting, sprinting would have been required to capture the animal. The animal would have to be carried back to camp to cook and eat. This would probably have required all the Primal Pattern® Movements, including gait (walking).

There are three distinct speeds of gait: walking, running (including jogging), and sprinting. Many sports involve the need for all three. Each speed of gait has a different relative timing of generalized motor program, which is believed to have been crucial to surviving in the wild. The difference in relative timing of the motor programs is crucial to an athlete's training routine. Remember that the training must closely resemble the motor program of the chosen sport to achieve maximum carry-over into the competitive arena. The specific relative timing of many power, agility, plyometric, and speed-training exercises like those in this book are essential to any athlete who has to run as part of their sport.

Within gait there are two main phases: the stance phase and the swing phase. The stance phase includes a heel strike, foot flat, mid-stance, heel-off, and toe-off. The stance phase can also be divided into contact, mid-stance, and propulsive phases. The swing phase includes acceleration, mid-swing, and deceleration.

Fast and efficient running requires good muscle balance (see pages 21–22), and good strength and co-ordination of all the muscles of the inner and outer unit of the core (see pages 48–54) and the other muscles that rotate the torso and move the limbs, particularly the shoulder and hip extensors. Any muscle imbalance will create what is known as "power leaks," which will lead to a reduction in force production and efficiency, and therefore reduce top speed and use more energy at relative speeds. Muscle imbalance can also lead to reciprocal inhibition (see glossary, page 135), and injury to the synergistically dominant (see glossary, page 135) muscles.

As running involves rotation of the torso, and flexion and extension of the limbs, all the exercises that strengthen the Primal Pattern® Movements from a standing position should also carry over to and increase running speed. It is important, however, that you carefully periodize your program (see pages 132–133) to achieve optimal speed and reduce the likelihood of injury.

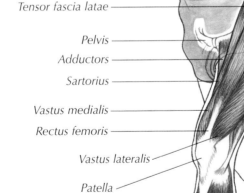

Tensor fascia latae

Pelvis

Adductors

Sartorius

Vastus medialis

Rectus femoris

Vastus lateralis

Patella

Tibialis anterior

Gluteus maximus

Gluteus medius

Biceps femoris

Gastrocnemius

Peroneus longus

Peroneus brevis

Soleus

LUNGE—BEGINNER
SPLIT SQUAT (STATIC LUNGE)

Basic description:
- Inhale and gently draw the navel toward the spine.
- Lower your body down to the ground.
- Allow the knees to bend and finish with the back knee about one inch from the floor.
- Keep most of the weight on the front leg.
- At the bottom of the lunge, drive back up by driving the front heel through the floor, exhaling through pursed lips as you pass through the most difficult part of the ascent.

Tips for good form:
- Keep the torso upright, gently squeeze your shoulder blades together and keep your head level with the horizon.
- Keep the front knee in line with the second toe as you descend and ascend. Do not allow the foot, ankle, or knee to move toward the mid-line.
- Keep your weight on the mid- to rear portion of your front foot.

STARTING POSITION
- Begin with hands on hips and your torso upright.
- Take a long stride forward with one leg.

Rectus femoris

Vastus intermedius

Vastus lateralis

Peroneus longus

Soleus

Peroneus brevis

Gluteus medius

Gluteus maximus

Biceps femoris

Gastrocnemius

ANALYSIS OF MOVEMENT	JOINTS	JOINT MOVEMENT	MOBILIZING MUSCLES
Joint 1	Hip	Down: flexion Up: extension	Front leg: Gluteus maximus, gluteus medius (posterior fibers), biceps femoris, semitendinosus, semimembranosus, adductor magnus (posterior fibers)
Joint 2	Knee	Down: flexion Up: extension	Front leg: Rectus femoris, vastus medialis, vastus intermedius, vastus lateralis
Joint 3	Ankle	Down: dorsiflexion Up: plantarflexion	Front leg: Gastrocnemius, soleus, tibialis posterior, peroneus longus and brevis

LUNGE—INTERMEDIATE
LUNGE

Basic description:

· Inhale, gently drawing the navel toward the spine.
· Take a large step forward and lower the body down to the ground under control.
· Allow the knees to bend and finish with the back knee about one inch from the floor.
· Keep most of the weight on the front leg.
· At the bottom of the lunge, drive straight back up to the starting position by driving the front heel through the floor, exhaling through pursed lips as you pass through the most difficult part of the ascent.

Tips for good form:

· Keep the torso upright, gently squeeze your shoulder blades together and keep your head level with the horizon.
· Keep the front knee in line with the second toe as you descend and ascend. Do not allow the foot, ankle, or knee to move toward the mid-line.
· Keep your weight on the mid- to rear portion of your front foot.

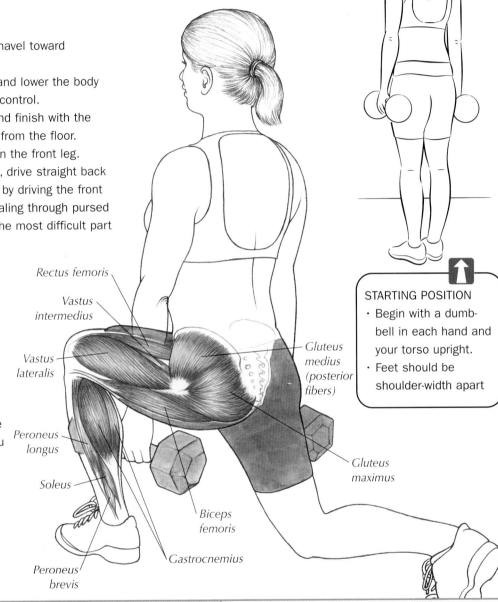

Rectus femoris
Vastus intermedius
Vastus lateralis
Peroneus longus
Soleus
Peroneus brevis
Gastrocnemius
Biceps femoris
Gluteus medius (posterior fibers)
Gluteus maximus

STARTING POSITION
· Begin with a dumb-bell in each hand and your torso upright.
· Feet should be shoulder-width apart

ANALYSIS OF MOVEMENT	JOINTS	JOINT MOVEMENT	MOBILIZING MUSCLES
Joint 1	Hip	Down: flexion Up: extension	Front leg: Gluteus maximus, gluteus medius (posterior fibers), biceps femoris, semitendinosus, semimembranosus, adductor magnus (posterior fibers)
Joint 2	Knee	Down: flexion Up: extension	Front leg: Rectus femoris, vastus medialis, vastus intermedius, vastus lateralis
Joint 3	Ankle	Down: dorsiflexion Up: plantarflexion	Front leg: Gastrocnemius, soleus, tibialis posterior, peroneus longus and brevis

LUNGE—ADVANCED
LUNGE ON BALL

Basic description:
- Inhale, gently drawing the navel toward the spine.
- Lower your body down to the ground.
- Allow the knees to bend, and finish with the back knee about one inch from the floor. If the ball prevents this, move the ball farther behind you.
- Keep most of your weight on the front leg.
- At the bottom of the lunge, drive back up by driving the front heel through the floor, exhaling through pursed lips as you pass through the most difficult part of the ascent.

STARTING POSITION
- Begin with hands on hips or a dumb-bell in each hand, with your torso upright.
- Place your back leg behind you on a swiss ball.

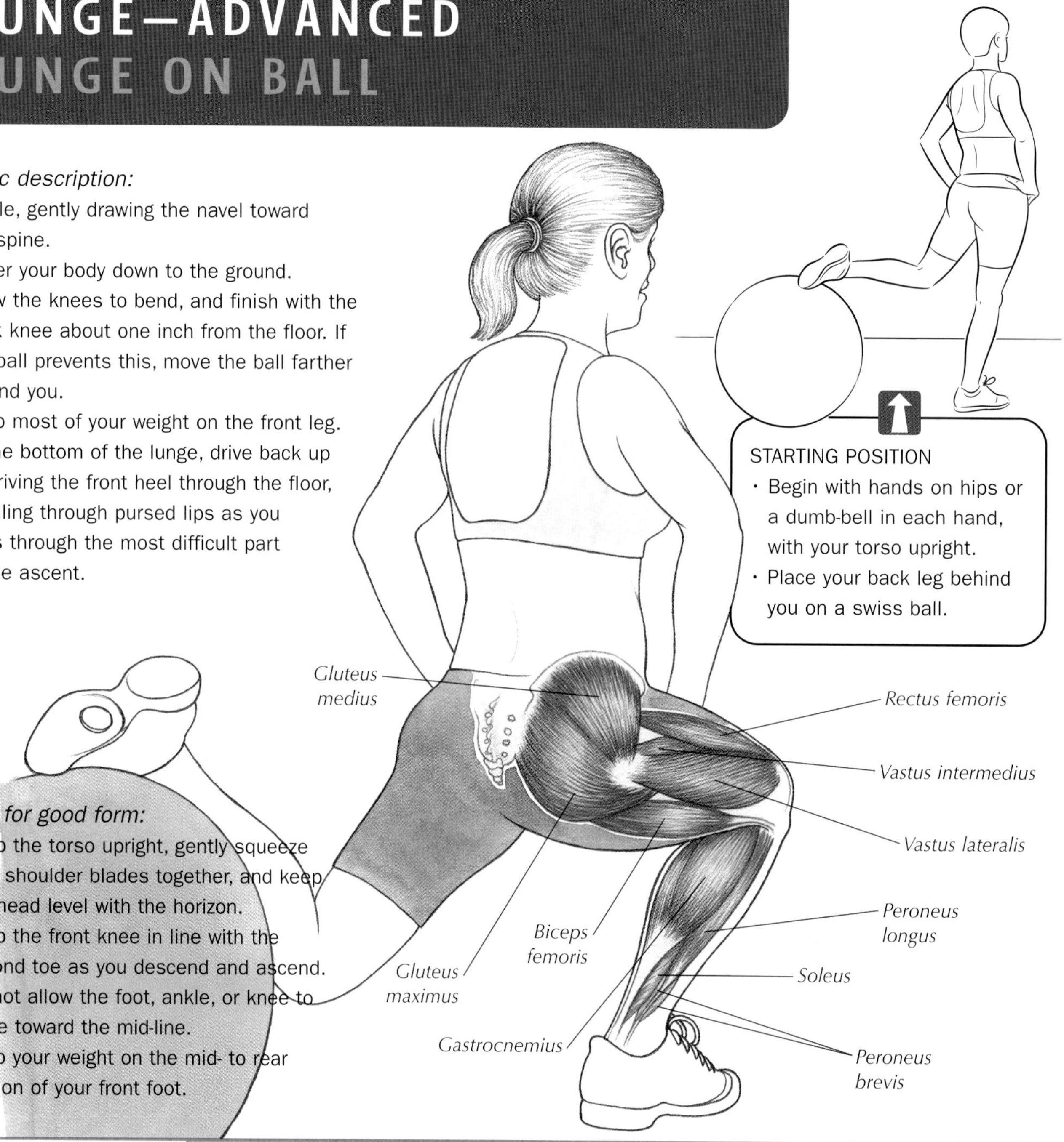

Tips for good form:
- Keep the torso upright, gently squeeze your shoulder blades together, and keep the head level with the horizon.
- Keep the front knee in line with the second toe as you descend and ascend.
- Do not allow the foot, ankle, or knee to move toward the mid-line.
- Keep your weight on the mid- to rear portion of your front foot.

Gluteus medius

Rectus femoris

Vastus intermedius

Vastus lateralis

Peroneus longus

Biceps femoris

Soleus

Gluteus maximus

Gastrocnemius

Peroneus brevis

ANALYSIS OF MOVEMENT	JOINTS	JOINT MOVEMENT	MOBILIZING MUSCLES
Joint 1	Hip	Down: flexion Up: extension	Front leg: Gluteus maximus, gluteus medius (posterior fibers), biceps femoris, semitendinosus, semimembranosus, adductor magnus (posterior fibers)
Joint 2	Knee	Down: flexion Up: extension	Front leg: Rectus femoris, vastus medialis, vastus intermedius, vastus lateralis
Joint 3	Ankle	Down: dorsiflexion Up: plantarflexion	Front leg: Gastrocnemius, soleus, tibialis posterior, peroneus longus and brevis

SQUAT—BEGINNER
WALL SQUAT

Tips for good form:
- Keep the torso upright, looking straight ahead.
- Keep the knees in line with the second toe on each foot.

STARTING POSITION
- Stand with your torso upright and eyes looking straight ahead, with or without dumb-bells.
- Place a swiss ball between your lower back and a solid wall.
- Feet should be shoulder-width apart and can be turned out up to 30°.

Basic description:
- Inhale, gently drawing the navel in toward the spine.
- Descend into a squat position, like sitting in a chair, as far as you can without rounding (flexing) your lumbar spine.
- At the bottom of the squat, drive your heels through the floor to push yourself back up.
- Exhale through the most challenging part of the ascent.

Labels: Adductor magnus, Semimembranosus, Gastrocnemius, Soleus, Semitendinosus, Peroneus longus, Peroneus brevis, Patella, Gluteus medius, Pelvis, Gluteus maximus, Rectus femoris, Vastus lateralis, Vastus intermedius (underneath), Vastus medialis, Gastrocnemius, Quadriceps group

ANALYSIS OF MOVEMENT	JOINTS	JOINT MOVEMENT	MOBILIZING MUSCLES
Joint 1	Hip	Down: flexion Up: extension	Gluteus maximus, gluteus medius (posterior fibers), biceps femoris, semitendinosus, semimembranosus, adductor magnus (posterior fibers)
Joint 2	Knee	Down: flexion Up: extension	Rectus femoris, vastus medialis, vastus intermedius, vastus lateralis
Joint 3	Ankle	Down: dorsiflexion Up: plantarflexion	Gastrocnemius, soleus, tibialis posterior, peroneus longus and brevis

SQUAT—INTERMEDIATE
FRONT SQUAT

Tips for good form:
· Keep the torso upright, looking straight ahead.
· Keep the knees in line with the second toe on each foot.

STARTING POSITION
· Stand with your torso upright and eyes looking straight ahead, with a dumb-bell held at shoulder height in front of the body with elbows up.
· Feet should be shoulder-width apart and can be turned out up to 30°.

Gastrocnemius

Vastus lateralis

Rectus femoris

Vastus intermedius

Gluteus medius

Peroneus longus

Peroneus brevis

Vastus lateralis

Soleus

Gluteus maximus

Basic description:
· Inhale, gently drawing the navel in toward the spine.
· Descend into a squat position, like sitting in a chair, as far as you can without rounding (flexing) your lumbar spine.
· At the bottom of the squat, drive your heels through the floor to push yourself back up.
· Exhale through the most challenging part of the ascent.

ANALYSIS OF MOVEMENT	JOINTS	JOINT MOVEMENT	MOBILIZING MUSCLES
Joint 1	Hip	Down: flexion Up: extension	Gluteus maximus, gluteus medius (posterior fibers), biceps femoris, semitendinosus, semimembranosus, adductor magnus (posterior fibers)
Joint 2	Knee	Down: flexion Up: extension	Rectus femoris, vastus medialis, vastus intermedius, vastus lateralis
Joint 3	Ankle	Down: dorsiflexion Up: plantarflexion	Gastrocnemius, soleus, tibialis posterior, peroneus longus and brevis

SQUAT—ADVANCED
SINGLE LEG SQUAT

Basic description:
- Inhale, gently drawing the navel in toward the spine.
- Descend into a squat position, like sitting in a chair, as far as you can without rounding (flexing) your lumbar spine.
- At the bottom of the squat, drive your heels through the floor to push yourself back up.
- Exhale through the most challenging part of the ascent.

Tips for good form:
- Keep the torso upright, looking straight ahead.
- Keep the knee of the standing leg in line with the second toe of the foot.

STARTING POSITION
- Stand on one leg with your torso upright and eyes looking straight ahead.
- Place your hands on opposite shoulders—you can hold dumb-bells or use a barbell.

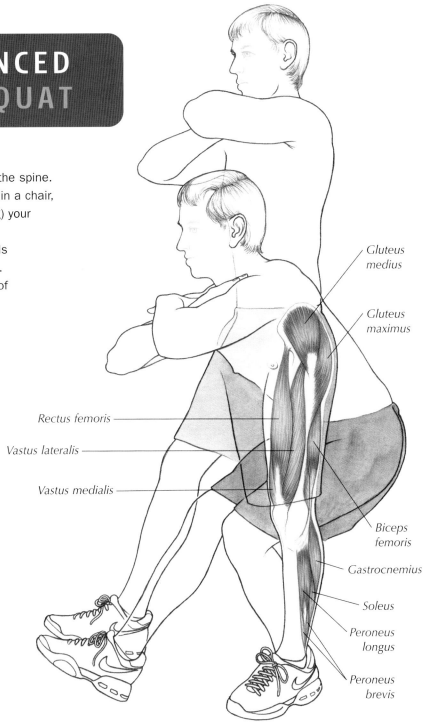

Gluteus medius

Gluteus maximus

Rectus femoris

Vastus lateralis

Vastus medialis

Biceps femoris

Gastrocnemius

Soleus

Peroneus longus

Peroneus brevis

ANALYSIS OF MOVEMENT	JOINTS	JOINT MOVEMENT	MOBILIZING MUSCLES
Joint 1	Hip	Down: flexion Up: extension	Standing leg: Gluteus maximus, gluteus medius (posterior fibers), biceps femoris, semitendinosus, semimembranosus, adductor magnus (posterior fibers)
Joint 2	Knee	Down: flexion Up: extension	Standing leg: Rectus femoris, vastus medialis, vastus intermedius, vastus lateralis
Joint 3	Ankle	Down: dorsiflexion Up: plantarflexion	Standing leg: Gastrocnemius, soleus, tibialis posterior, peroneus longus and brevis

BEND—BEGINNER ROMANIAN DEADLIFT (STIFF-LEG DEADLIFT)

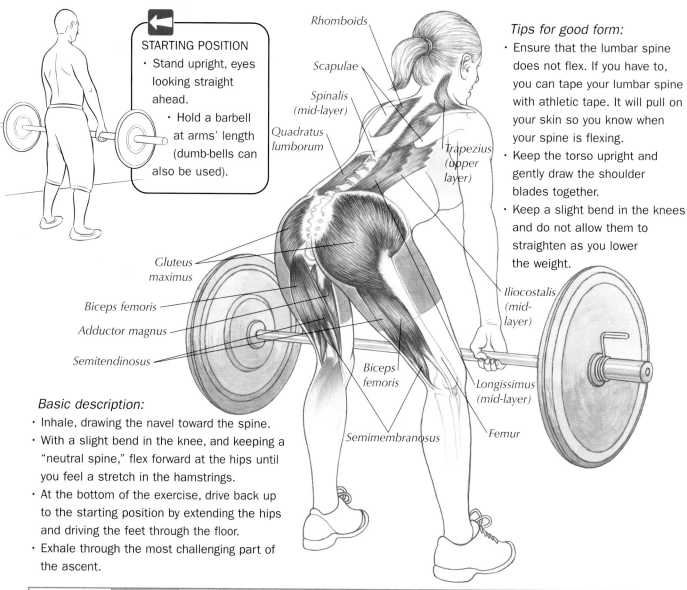

STARTING POSITION
- Stand upright, eyes looking straight ahead.
- Hold a barbell at arms' length (dumb-bells can also be used).

Rhomboids

Scapulae

Spinalis (mid-layer)

Quadratus lumborum

Trapezius (upper layer)

Gluteus maximus

Biceps femoris

Adductor magnus

Semitendinosus

Iliocostalis (mid-layer)

Biceps femoris

Longissimus (mid-layer)

Semimembranosus

Femur

Tips for good form:
- Ensure that the lumbar spine does not flex. If you have to, you can tape your lumbar spine with athletic tape. It will pull on your skin so you know when your spine is flexing.
- Keep the torso upright and gently draw the shoulder blades together.
- Keep a slight bend in the knees and do not allow them to straighten as you lower the weight.

Basic description:
- Inhale, drawing the navel toward the spine.
- With a slight bend in the knee, and keeping a "neutral spine," flex forward at the hips until you feel a stretch in the hamstrings.
- At the bottom of the exercise, drive back up to the starting position by extending the hips and driving the feet through the floor.
- Exhale through the most challenging part of the ascent.

ANALYSIS OF MOVEMENT	JOINTS	JOINT MOVEMENT	MOBILIZING MUSCLES
Joint 1	Hip	Down: flexion Up: extension	Gluteus maximus, gluteus medius (posterior fibers), biceps femoris, semitendinosus, semimembranosus, adductor magnus (posterior fibers)
Joint 2	Lumbar spine	Stabilization: extension	Multifidus, spinalis, longissimus, iliocostalis, quadratus lumborum, interspinalis
Joint 3	Scapula	Adduction	Trapezius (middle fibers), rhomboid major and minor
Joint 4	Knee	Grip: flexion	Flexor carpi radialis, flexor carpi ulnaris, palmaris longus, flexor digitorum superficialis

BEND—INTERMEDIATE
DEADLIFT

Basic description:
- Inhale, drawing the navel toward the spine.
- Drive the feet through the floor to initiate the ascent, exhaling through pursed lips through the most challenging part of the lift. Keep the torso at the same angle until the weight passes the knees.
- Keep the weight as close to the body as possible as you lift.
- As soon as the weight passes the knees, drive the hips forward until you are standing upright. Keep your arms straight throughout.
- At the top of the exercise, keep the navel drawn in and inhale. Then descend the weight, keeping it close to the body by bending at the hips until the weight reaches the knees, then bend the knees until the weight reaches the floor.
- Exhale through the most challenging part of the ascent and the descent.

Tips for good form:
- Ensure that the lumbar spine does not flex. If you have to, you can tape your lumbar spine with athletic tape, so you know if your spine is flexing.
- Keep a neutral spine and gently draw the shoulder blades together.
- Keep your eyes level with the horizon.

> **STARTING POSITION**
> - A bent forward position with a barbell in front of you.
> - Grip the bar and keep the spine in good alignment.

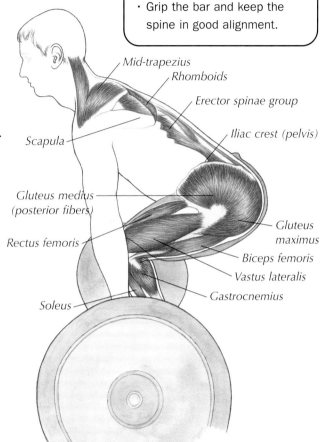

Mid-trapezius
Rhomboids
Erector spinae group
Iliac crest (pelvis)
Scapula
Gluteus medius (posterior fibers)
Gluteus maximus
Rectus femoris
Biceps femoris
Vastus lateralis
Gastrocnemius
Soleus

ANALYSIS OF MOVEMENT	JOINTS	JOINT MOVEMENT	MOBILIZING MUSCLES
Joint 1	Hip	Up: extension Down: flexion	Gluteus maximus, gluteus medius (posterior fibers), biceps femoris, semitendinosus, semimembranosus, adductor magnus (posterior fibers)
Joint 2	Knee	Up: extension Down: flexion	Rectus femoris, vastus medialis, vastus intermedius, vastus lateralis
Joint 3	Ankle	Up: upward rotation, abduction Down: downward rotation, adduction	Gastrocnemius, soleus, tibialis posterior, peroneus longus and brevis
Joint 4	Lumbar spine	Stabilization: extension	Multifidus, spinalis, longissimus, iliocostalis, quadratus lumborum, interspinalis
Joint 5	Scapula	Adduction	Trapezius (middle fibers), rhomboid major and minor
Joint 6	Wrist	Grip: flexion	Flexor carpi radialis, flexor carpi ulnaris, palmaris longus, flexor digitorum superficialis

BEND—ADVANCED
SINGLE LEG DEADLIFT

Basic description:
- Inhale, drawing the navel toward the spine.
- Drive your foot through the floor to initiate the ascent, exhaling through pursed lips through the most challenging part of the lift. Keep the torso at the same angle until the weight passes the knees.
- Keep the weight as close to the body as possible as you lift.
- As soon as the weight passes the knees, drive the hips forward until you are standing upright. Keep your arms straight throughout.
- At the top of the exercise, keep the navel drawn in and inhale. Then descend the weight, keeping it close to the body by bending at the hips until the weight reaches the knees, then bend the knees until the weight reaches the floor.
- Exhale through the most challenging part of the ascent and descent.

STARTING POSITION
- A bent forward position on one leg with a barbell in front of you. The "free" leg should be behind you.
- Grip the bar and keep the spine in good alignment.

Tips for good form:
- Ensure that the lumbar spine do not flex. If you have to, you can tape your lumbar spine with athletic tape, so you know if your spine is flexing.
- Keep the torso upright and gent draw the shoulder blades togeth
- Keep your eyes level with the horizon.

Scapula
Rhomboids
Trapezius (middle fibers)
Erector spinae group (lower section)
Gluteus medius (posterior fibers)
Quadratus lumborum
Gluteus maximus
Femur
Vastus lateralis
Biceps femoris
Semitendinosus

ANALYSIS OF MOVEMENT	JOINTS	JOINT MOVEMENT	MOBILIZING MUSCLES
Joint 1	Hip	Up: extension Down: flexion	Gluteus maximus and medius (posterior fibers), biceps femoris, semitendinosus, semimembranosus, adductor magnus (posterior)
Joint 2	Knee	Up: extension Down: flexion	Rectus femoris, vastus medialis, vastus intermedius, vastus lateralis
Joint 3	Ankle	Up: plantarflexion Down: dorsiflexion	Gastrocnemius, soleus, tibialis posterior, peroneus longus and brevis
Joint 4	Hip	Down: flexion Up: extension	Gluteus maximus, gluteus medius (posterior fibers), biceps femoris, semitendinosus, semimembranosus, adductor magnus (posterior)
Joint 5	Lumbar spine	Stabilization: extension	Multifidus, spinalis, longissimus, iliocostalis, quadratus lumborum, interspinalis

PULL—BEGINNER
SEATED CABLE PULL

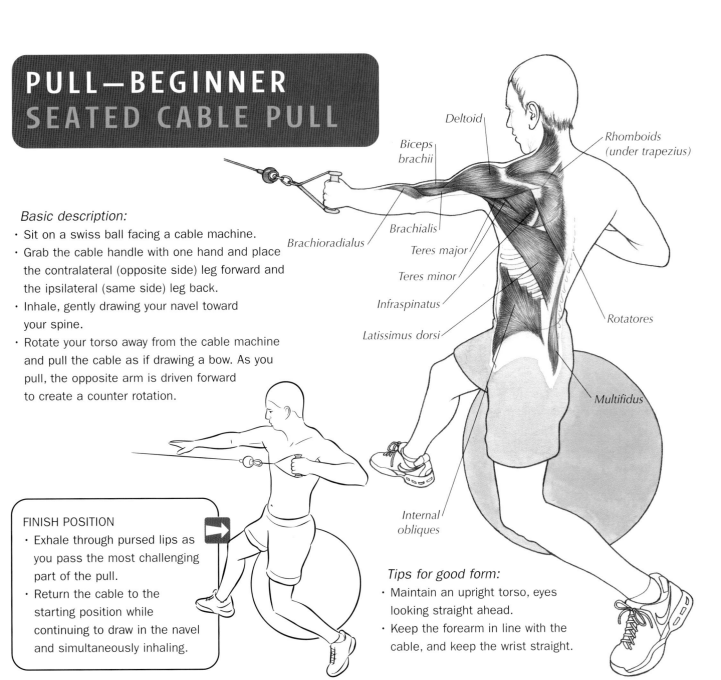

Basic description:
· Sit on a swiss ball facing a cable machine.
· Grab the cable handle with one hand and place the contralateral (opposite side) leg forward and the ipsilateral (same side) leg back.
· Inhale, gently drawing your navel toward your spine.
· Rotate your torso away from the cable machine and pull the cable as if drawing a bow. As you pull, the opposite arm is driven forward to create a counter rotation.

Deltoid
Biceps brachii
Rhomboids (under trapezius)
Brachioradialus
Brachialis
Teres major
Teres minor
Infraspinatus
Latissimus dorsi
Rotatores
Multifidus
Internal obliques

FINISH POSITION
· Exhale through pursed lips as you pass the most challenging part of the pull.
· Return the cable to the starting position while continuing to draw in the navel and simultaneously inhaling.

Tips for good form:
· Maintain an upright torso, eyes looking straight ahead.
· Keep the forearm in line with the cable, and keep the wrist straight.

ANALYSIS OF MOVEMENT	JOINTS	JOINT MOVEMENT	MOBILIZING MUSCLES
Joint 1	Spine	Rotation	Ipsilateral: Internal oblique Contralateral: Multifidus, rotatores, external oblique
Joint 2	Scapula	Pull: adduction Return: abduction	Trapezius (middle fibers), rhomboid major and minor
Joint 3	Shoulder	Pull: horizontal abduction, extension Return: horizontal adduction	Deltoid (posterior fibers), infraspinatus, teres minor, latissimus dorsi, teres major
Joint 4	Elbow	Pull: flexion Return: extension	Biceps brachii, brachialis, brachioradialis, flexor carpi radialis, palmaris
Joint 5	Forearm	Pull: supination Return: pronation	Biceps brachii, supinator

Basic description:

- Inhale, gently drawing your navel toward your spine.
- Push off the front heel, driving your body weight away from the machine, rotate your torso away from the machine, and pull the cable as if drawing a bow. As you pull, the opposite arm is driven forward to create a counter rotation.
- Exhale through pursed lips as you pass the most challenging part of the pull.
- Return the cable to the starting position while maintaining the drawing in of the navel and simultaneously inhaling.

STARTING POSITION
- Stand facing a cable machine, in a low lunge position.
- Grab the cable handle with the hand contralateral to the forward leg.

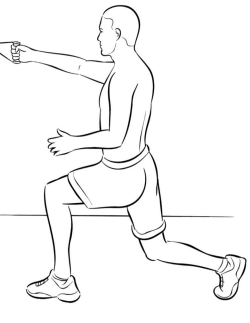

ANALYSIS OF MOVEMENT	JOINTS	JOINT MOVEMENT	MOBILIZING MUSCLES
Joint 1	Ankle	Front: plantarflexion Back: dorsiflexion	Front foot: Gastrocnemius, soleus, tibialis posterior, peroneus longus and brevis
Joint 2	Knee	Front: extension	Rectus femoris, vastus medialis, vastus intermedius, vastus lateralis
Joint 3	Hip	Front: extension Back: external rotation	Front: gluteus maximus, gluteus medius (posterior fibers), biceps femoris, semitendinosus, semimembranosus, adductor magnus (posterior fibers) Back: gluteus maximus, gluteus medius (posterior fibers), biceps femoris, sartorius, psoas, iliacus, piriformis, quadratus femoris, gemellus superior and inferior, obturator externus and internus
Joint 4	Spine	Rotation	Ipsilateral: Internal oblique Contralateral: Multifidus, rotatores, external oblique
Joint 5	Scapula	Pull: adduction Return: abduction	Trapezius (middle fibers), rhomboid major and minor
Joint 6	Shoulder	Pull: horizontal abduction, extension Return: horizontal adduction	Deltoid (posterior fibers), infraspinatus, teres minor, latissimus dorsi, teres major
Joint 7	Elbow	Pull: flexion Return: extension	Biceps brachii, brachialis, brachioradialis, flexor carpi radialis, palmaris
Joint 8	Forearm	Pull: supination Return: pronation	Biceps brachii, supinator

Peroneus br

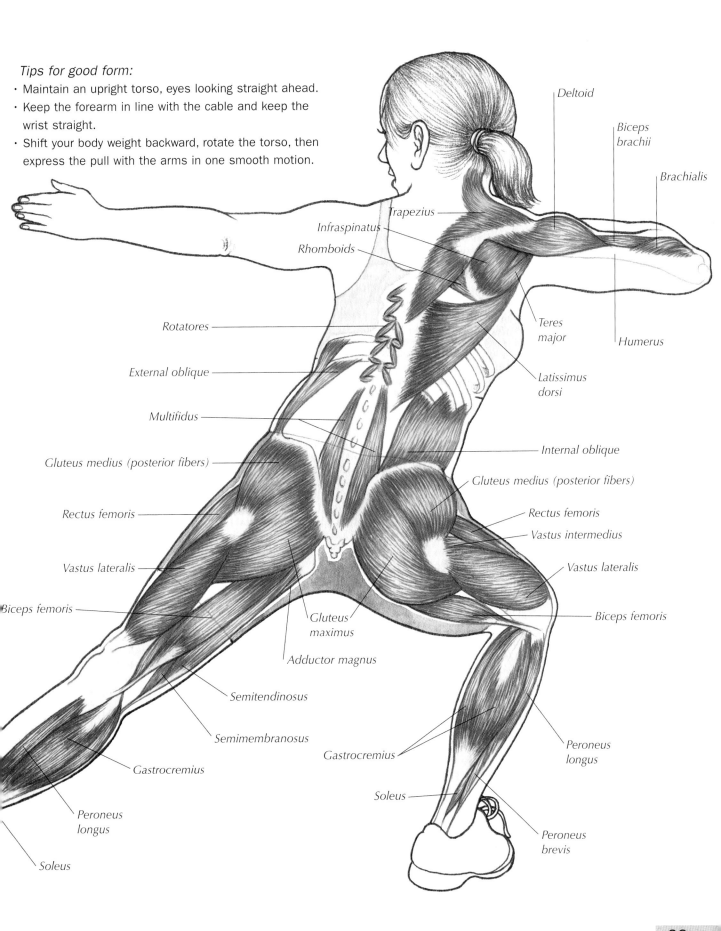

Tips for good form:
- Maintain an upright torso, eyes looking straight ahead.
- Keep the forearm in line with the cable and keep the wrist straight.
- Shift your body weight backward, rotate the torso, then express the pull with the arms in one smooth motion.

Deltoid

Biceps brachii

Brachialis

Trapezius

Infraspinatus

Rhomboids

Teres major

Humerus

Rotatores

Latissimus dorsi

External oblique

Multifidus

Internal oblique

Gluteus medius (posterior fibers)

Gluteus medius (posterior fibers)

Rectus femoris

Rectus femoris

Vastus intermedius

Vastus lateralis

Vastus lateralis

Biceps femoris

Biceps femoris

Gluteus maximus

Adductor magnus

Semitendinosus

Peroneus longus

Semimembranosus

Gastrocremius

Gastrocremius

Soleus

Peroneus longus

Peroneus brevis

Soleus

PULL—ADVANCED
SINGLE ARM, SINGLE LEG CABLE PULL

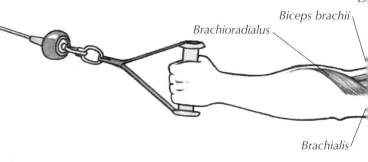

Biceps brachii
Brachioradialus
Brachialis

Basic description:
· Stand facing a cable machine on one leg, the other leg reaching out behind you.
· Lean forward from the hip without flexing the spine, grabbing the cable handle with the hand contralateral to the stance leg.
· Inhale, gently drawing your navel toward the spine.
· Push off the front heel, drive the pelvis forward, rotate the torso away from the machine and pull the cable as if drawing a bow. As you pull, the opposite leg comes forward with the knee bent at 90°, and the contralateral arm is driven forward to create a counter-rotation.

Tips for good form:
· Ensure that the spine does not go into flexion and keep your eyes looking straight ahead throughout.
· Keep the forearm in line with the cable and keep the wrist straight.

ANALYSIS OF MOVEMENT	JOINTS	JOINT MOVEMENT	MOBILIZING MUSCLES
Joint 1	Ankle	Front leg: plantarflexion	Front leg: Gastrocnemius, soleus, tibialis posterior, peroneus longus and brevis
Joint 2	Knee	Front leg: extension	Rectus femoris, vastus medialis, vastus intermedius, vastus lateralis
Joint 3	Hip	Front leg: extension Back: flexion	Front leg: Gluteus maximus, gluteus medius (posterior fibers), biceps femoris, semitendinosus, semimembranosus, adductor magnus (posterior fibers) Back leg: Psoas, iliacus, rectus femoris, tensor fascia lata, sartorius, adductor brevis, longus and magnus, gluteus medius (anterior fibers), gluteus minimus
Joint 4	Spine	Rotation	Ipsilateral: Internal oblique Contralateral: Multifidus, rotatores, external oblique
Joint 5	Scapula	Pull: adduction Return: abduction	Trapezius (middle fibers), rhomboid major and minor
Joint 6	Shoulder	Pull: horizontal abduction, extension Return: horizontal adduction	Deltoid (posterior fibers), infraspinatus, teres minor, latissimus dorsi, teres major
Joint 7	Elbow	Pull: flexion Return: extension	Biceps brachii, brachialis, brachioradialis, flexor carpi radialis, palmaris
Joint 8	Forearm	Pull: supination Return: pronation	Biceps brachii, supinator

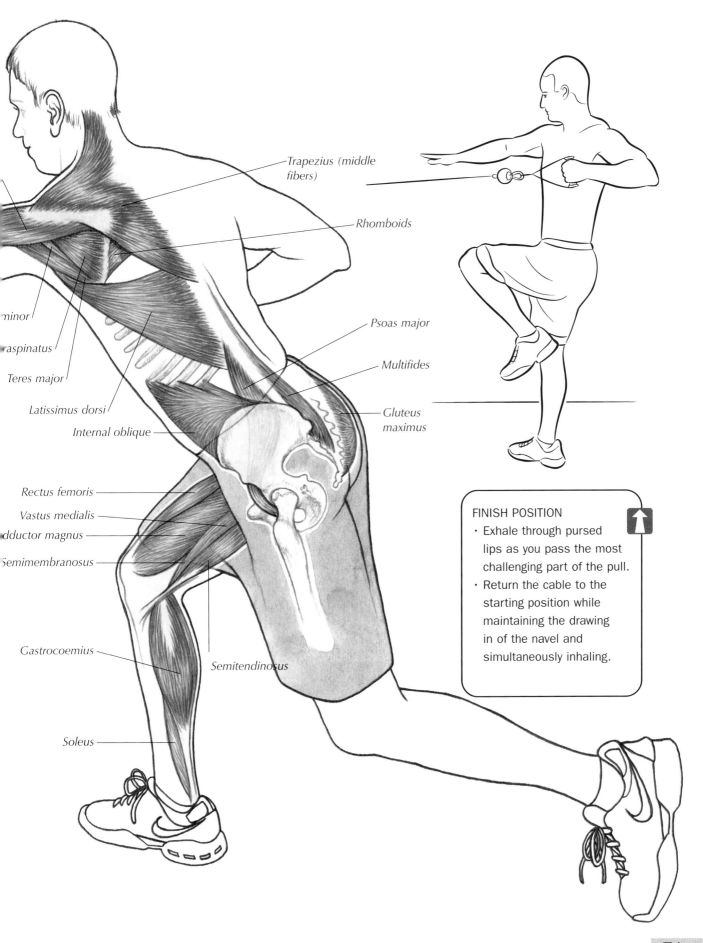

Trapezius (middle fibers)

Rhomboids

minor

raspinatus

Teres major

Latissimus dorsi

Internal oblique

Psoas major

Multifides

Gluteus maximus

Rectus femoris

Vastus medialis

dductor magnus

Semimembranosus

Gastrocoemius

Semitendinosus

Soleus

FINISH POSITION
· Exhale through pursed lips as you pass the most challenging part of the pull.
· Return the cable to the starting position while maintaining the drawing in of the navel and simultaneously inhaling.

Basic description:
- Sit on a swiss ball facing away from a cable machine.
- Grab the cable handle with one hand, and place the contralateral (opposite side) leg forward and the ipsilateral (same side) leg back.
- Inhale, gently drawing your navel toward your spine.
- Rotate your torso away from the cable machine and push the cable as if throwing a punch. As you push, the opposite arm is driven backward to create a counter-rotation.

Deltoid (anterior fibers)

Triceps brachii

Pectoralis major (upper fibers)

Anconeus

Internal oblique

Serratus anterior

External oblique

Tips for good form:
- Maintain an upright torso, eyes looking straight ahead.
- Keep the forearm in line with the cable and keep the wrist straight.

FINISH POSITION
- Exhale through pursed lips as you pass the most challenging part of the push.
- Return the cable to the starting position while maintaining drawing in the navel and simultaneously inhaling.

ANALYSIS OF MOVEMENT	JOINTS	JOINT MOVEMENT	MOBILIZING MUSCLES
Joint 1	Spine	Rotation	Ipsilateral: Internal oblique Contralateral: Multifidus, rotatores, external oblique
Joint 2	Scapula	Push: abduction Return: abduction	Pectoralis minor, serratus anterior
Joint 3	Shoulder	Push: horizontal abduction, extension Return: horizontal adduction	Deltoid (anterior fibers), pectoralis major (upper fibers)
Joint 4	Elbow	Push: extension Return: flexion	Triceps brachii, anconeus
Joint 5	Forearm	Push: pronation Return: supination	Pronator teres, pronator quadratus

Tips for good form:
· Maintain an upright torso, eyes looking straight ahead.
· Keep the forearm in line with the cable, and keep the wrist straight.
· Shift your body weight forward, rotate the torso, then express the push with the arms in one smooth movement.

STARTING POSITION
· Stand facing away from a cable machine, in a low side-lunge position.
· Grab the cable handle with the hand contralateral to the forward leg (for safety reasons grab the handle before you get into the side-lunge position).

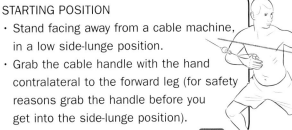

Basic description:
· Inhale, gently drawing your navel toward your spine.
· Push off the back foot, driving your body weight away from the machine. Rotate the torso away from the machine and push the cable as if throwing a punch. As you push, the opposite arm is driven backward to create a counter-rotation.
· Exhale through pursed lips as you pass the most challenging part of the push.
· Return the cable to the start position while maintaining the drawing in of the navel and simultaneously inhaling.

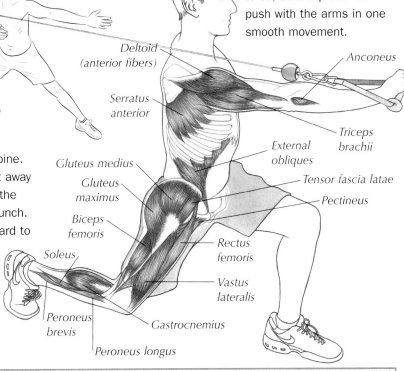

Deltoid (anterior fibers)
Serratus anterior
Gluteus medius
Gluteus maximus
Biceps femoris
Soleus
Peroneus brevis
Peroneus longus
Gastrocnemius
Rectus femoris
Vastus lateralis
Pectineus
Tensor fascia latae
External obliques
Triceps brachii
Anconeus

ANALYSIS OF MOVEMENT	JOINTS	JOINT MOVEMENT	MOBILIZING MUSCLES
Joint 1	Ankle	Back leg: plantarflexion Front leg: dorsiflexion	Back leg: Gastrocnemius, soleus, tibialis posterior, peroneus longus and brevis
Joint 2	Knee	Back leg: extension Front leg: flexion	Back leg: Rectus femoris, vastus medialis, vastus intermedius, vastus lateralis
Joint 3	Hip	Back leg: extension, internal rotation Front leg: flexion, internal rotation	Back leg: Gluteus maximus, gluteus medius (posterior fibers), biceps femoris, semitendinosus, semimembranosus, gluteus medius (anterior fibers), gluteus minimus, pectineus, adductor brevis, longus and magnus, gracilis, tensor fascia lata
Joint 4	Spine	Rotation	Ipsilateral: Internal oblique Contralateral: Multifidus, rotatores, external oblique
Joint 5	Scapula	Push: abduction Return: adduction	Pectoralis minor, serratus anterior
Joint 6	Shoulder	Push: horizontal adduction Return: horizontal abduction	Deltoid (anterior fibers), pectoralis major (upper fibers)
Joint 7	Elbow	Push: extension Return: flexion	Triceps brachii, anconeus
Joint 8	Forearm	Push: pronation Return: supination	Pronator teres, pronator quadratus

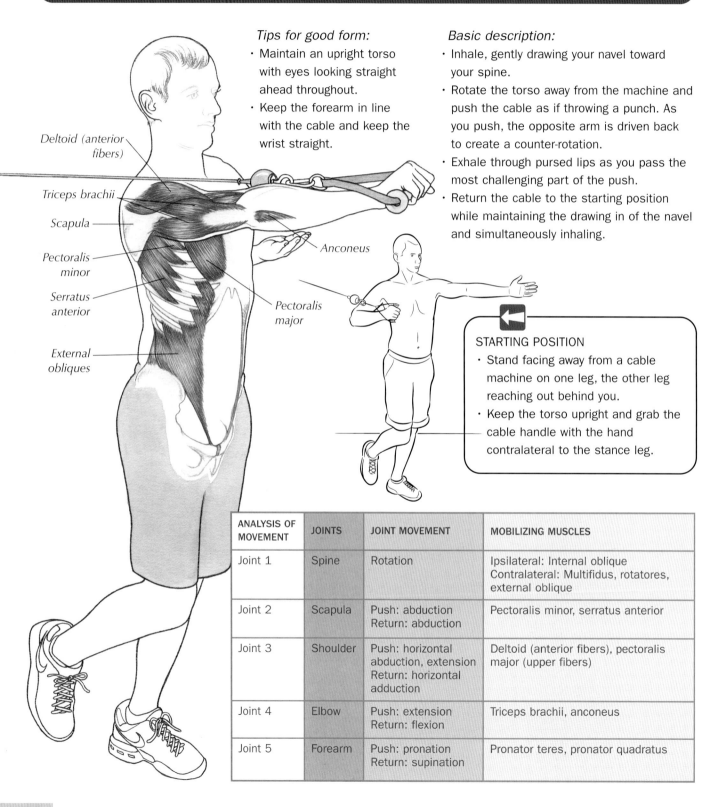

Deltoid (anterior fibers)

Triceps brachii

Scapula

Pectoralis minor

Serratus anterior

External obliques

Anconeus

Pectoralis major

Tips for good form:
- Maintain an upright torso with eyes looking straight ahead throughout.
- Keep the forearm in line with the cable and keep the wrist straight.

Basic description:
- Inhale, gently drawing your navel toward your spine.
- Rotate the torso away from the machine and push the cable as if throwing a punch. As you push, the opposite arm is driven back to create a counter-rotation.
- Exhale through pursed lips as you pass the most challenging part of the push.
- Return the cable to the starting position while maintaining the drawing in of the navel and simultaneously inhaling.

STARTING POSITION
- Stand facing away from a cable machine on one leg, the other leg reaching out behind you.
- Keep the torso upright and grab the cable handle with the hand contralateral to the stance leg.

ANALYSIS OF MOVEMENT	JOINTS	JOINT MOVEMENT	MOBILIZING MUSCLES
Joint 1	Spine	Rotation	Ipsilateral: Internal oblique Contralateral: Multifidus, rotatores, external oblique
Joint 2	Scapula	Push: abduction Return: abduction	Pectoralis minor, serratus anterior
Joint 3	Shoulder	Push: horizontal abduction, extension Return: horizontal adduction	Deltoid (anterior fibers), pectoralis major (upper fibers)
Joint 4	Elbow	Push: extension Return: flexion	Triceps brachii, anconeus
Joint 5	Forearm	Push: pronation Return: supination	Pronator teres, pronator quadratus

TWIST—BEGINNER
SEATED WOOD CHOP

Basic description:

· Sit upright on a swiss ball facing away from a cable
  machine.
· Grip the cable handle with the hand farthest away
  from it, and place the other hand over the
  top of the gripping hand.
· Inhale, gently drawing your navel toward your spine.
· Rotate the torso away from the cable machine, taking
  the cable handle with you as if chopping wood.

Tips for good form:

· Maintain an upright torso,
  eyes looking straight ahead.
· Maintain a slight bend in
  the elbows.

FINISH POSITION
· Exhale through pursed lips as
  you pass the most challenging
  part of the twist.
· Return the cable to the starting
  position, maintaining the drawing
  in of the navel and
  simultaneously inhaling.

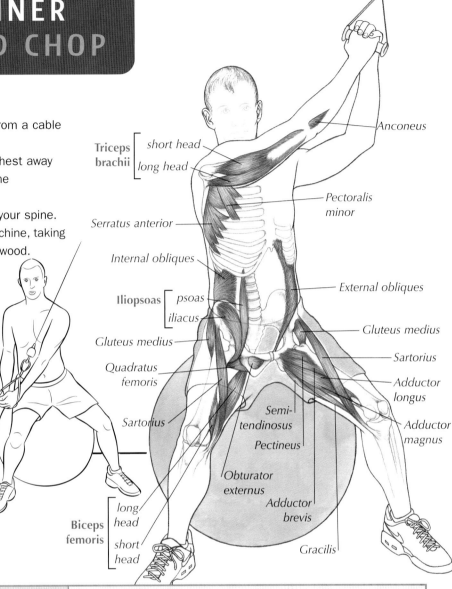

Anconeus

Triceps brachii — short head / long head

Pectoralis minor

Serratus anterior

Internal obliques

External obliques

Iliopsoas — psoas / iliacus

Gluteus medius

Gluteus medius

Sartorius

Quadratus femoris

Adductor longus

Semi-tendinosus

Sartorius

Adductor magnus

Pectineus

Obturator externus

Adductor brevis

Biceps femoris — long head / short head

Gracilis

ANALYSIS OF MOVEMENT	JOINTS	JOINT MOVEMENT	MOBILIZING MUSCLES
Joint 1	Spine	Rotation	Ipsilateral: Internal oblique Contralateral: Multifidus, rotatores, external oblique
Joint 2	Scapula	Downward rotation, upward rotation, adduction, abduction, elevation, depression	Trapezius (upper and lower fibers), pectoralis minor, serratus anterior
Joint 3	Shoulder	Extension, flexion	Latissimus dorsi, teres major
Joint 4	Hip	Internal rotation, lateral rotation	Inside leg: Gluteus medius (anterior fibers), gluteus minimus, pectineus, adductor brevis, longus and magnus, gracilis, tensor fascia lata, semitendinosus, semimembranosus Outside leg: Gluteus maximus, gluteus medius (posterior fibers), biceps femoris, sartorius, psoas, iliacus, piriformis, quadratus femoris, gemellus superior and inferior, obturator externus and internus

TWIST—INTERMEDIATE
WOOD CHOP

Basic description:

· Stand facing away from a cable machine, in a side-lunge position with 70 percent of your weight on the inside leg.

· Grab the cable handle with the hand farthest from the machine. Place the hand closest on top of your other hand.

· Inhale, gently drawing your navel toward the spine.

· Push off the foot closest to the cable, driving your body weight away from the machine. Rotate the torso away from the machine and twist the cable as if chopping wood.

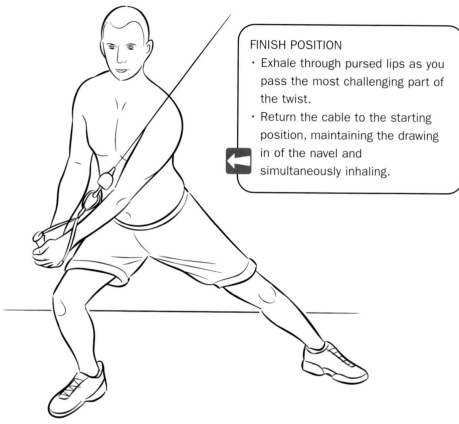

FINISH POSITION

· Exhale through pursed lips as you pass the most challenging part of the twist.

· Return the cable to the starting position, maintaining the drawing in of the navel and simultaneously inhaling.

ANALYSIS OF MOVEMENT	JOINTS	JOINT MOVEMENT	MOBILIZING MUSCLES
Joint 1	Spine	Rotation	Ipsilateral: Internal oblique Contralateral: Multifidus, rotatores, external oblique
Joint 2	Scapula	Downward rotation, upward rotation, adduction, abduction, elevation, depression	Trapezius (upper and lower fibers), pectoralis minor, serratus anterior
Joint 3	Shoulder	Extension, flexion	Latissimus dorsi, teres major
Joint 4	Hip	Internal rotation, lateral rotation, abduction, adduction	Inside leg: Gluteus maximus, gluteus medius, gluteus minimus, tensor fascia lata, sartorius, pectineus, adductor brevis, longus and magnus, gracilis, tensor fascia lata, semitendinosus, semimembranosus Outside leg: Gluteus maximus, gluteus medius (posterior fibers), biceps femoris, sartorius, psoas, iliacus, piriformis, quadratus femoris, gemellus superior and inferior, obturator externus and internus
Joint 5	Knee	Extension, flexion	Rectus femoris, vastus medialis, vastus intermedius, vastus lateralis
Joint 6	Ankle	Plantarflexion, dorsiflexion	Gastrocnemius, soleus, tibialis posterior, peroneus longus and brevisicialis

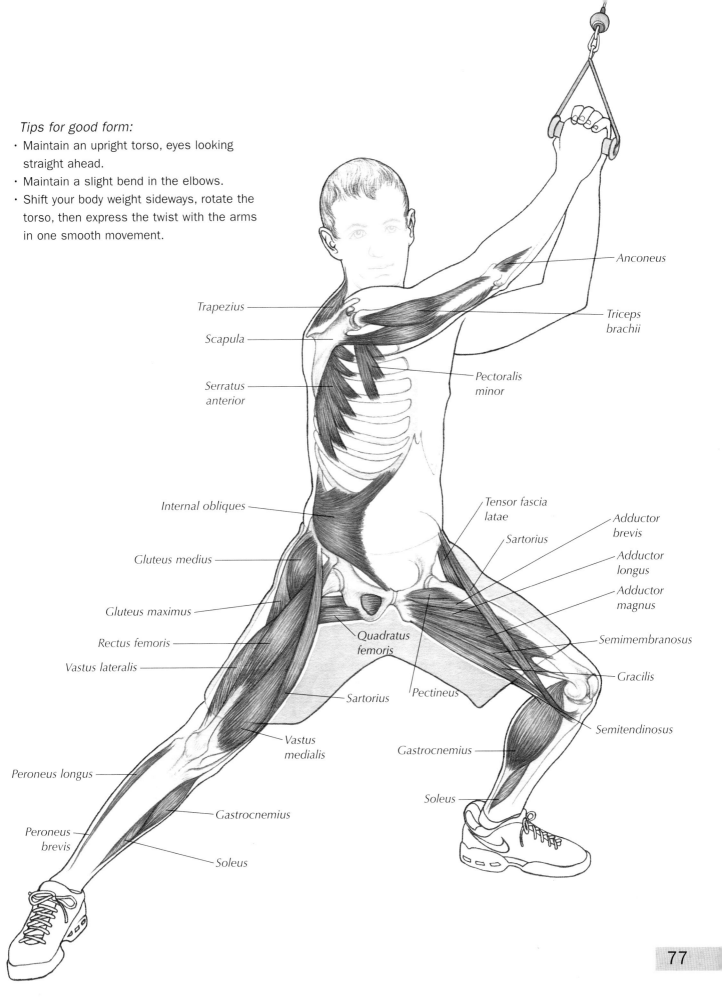

Tips for good form:
· Maintain an upright torso, eyes looking
  straight ahead.
· Maintain a slight bend in the elbows.
· Shift your body weight sideways, rotate the
  torso, then express the twist with the arms
  in one smooth movement.

Trapezius

Scapula

*Serratus
anterior*

Internal obliques

Gluteus medius

Gluteus maximus

Rectus femoris

Vastus lateralis

Sartorius

*Vastus
medialis*

Peroneus longus

*Peroneus
brevis*

Gastrocnemius

Soleus

*Quadratus
femoris*

Pectineus

Anconeus

*Triceps
brachii*

*Pectoralis
minor*

*Tensor fascia
latae*

Sartorius

*Adductor
brevis*

*Adductor
longus*

*Adductor
magnus*

Semimembranosus

Gracilis

Semitendinosus

Gastrocnemius

Soleus

TWIST—ADVANCED
SINGLE LEG WOOD CHOP

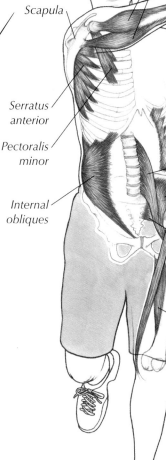

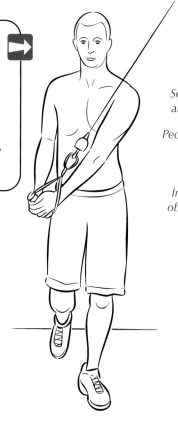

FINISH POSITION
- Exhale through pursed lips as you pass the most challenging part of the twist.
- Return the cable to the starting position, maintaining the drawing in of the navel and simultaneously inhaling.

Triceps brachii

Scapula

Anconeus

Serratus anterior

Pectoralis minor

External obliques

psoas
iliacus } Iliopsoas

Internal obliques

Gluteus medius

Pelvis

Piriformis

Femur

Biceps femoris

Basic description:
- Stand facing away from a cable machine on one leg, the other leg off the floor behind you.
- Keep the torso upright, grab the cable handle with the hand farthest away from it and place the other hand on top.
- Inhale, gently drawing your navel toward your spine
- Rotate the torso away from the machine and twist the cable as if chopping down a tree.

Tips for good form:
- Maintain an upright torso and keep your eyes looking straight ahead throughout.
- Maintain a slight bend in the elbows.

ANALYSIS OF MOVEMENT	JOINTS	JOINT MOVEMENT	MOBILIZING MUSCLES
Joint 1	Spine	Rotation	Ipsilateral: Internal oblique Contralateral: Multifidus, rotatores, external oblique
Joint 2	Shoulder	Downward rotation, upward rotation, adduction, abduction, elevation, depression	Latissimus dorsi, teres major, deltoid (posterior fibers), teres minor, triceps (long head)
Joint 3	Scapula	Extension, flexion	Triceps brachii, anconeus
Joint 4	Hip	External rotation, internal rotation	Standing leg: Gluteus maximus, gluteus medius (posterior fibers), biceps femoris, sartorius, psoas, iliacus, piriformis, quadratus femoris, gemellus superior and inferior, obturator externus and internus

Strength

In simple terms, strength can be defined as "the ability to exert a maximal force against a resistance" (H. Newton, *Explosive Lifting for Sports*).

Strength development can be split into two important categories: absolute and relative strength. Absolute strength is where there is no concern for body size. For example, linemen in American football, forwards in rugby, heavyweight boxers, and sumo wrestlers have no concern for their weight, they just need to become as strong as possible. Relative strength however, has a weight factor involved. For instance, a weight category boxer, a weightlifter, an endurance athlete, or an ice dancer (where extra weight will expend more energy) will want to gain strength without gaining size or weight. Therefore, relative strength is a requirement to improve strength relative to body weight. You need to determine whether you require absolute or relative strength, which will determine how you select exercise variables (see page 124).

Newton's second law of motion states that "f = ma," where "f" equals the amount of force available, "m" equals the mass involved, and "a" is the amount of acceleration available to move the mass. While it could be said that acceleration is ultimately more important than flat-out speed in most sports, the amount of force required to generate acceleration is limited by the strength required to generate that force. The more strength you gain, the more you can accelerate a mass, as long as you train acceleration too. Therefore, you also need to factor in how much acceleration your sport requires, which will also have a bearing on the strength you need to develop.

So how much strength do you need? This all depends on the mass that you need to overcome. If you play rugby, judo, or wrestling, or are an Olympic weightlifter, you will be required to overcome the mass of an opponent, sometimes much bigger than you, or to lift huge loads overhead. Therefore, the strength requirement will be high. If you are a racket sport player, golfer, swimmer, or soccer player, the strength requirement will be relatively low.

There comes a point where getting stronger will no longer lead to gains in your performance and will restrict recovery time or limit time spent on other, more important, biomotor abilities. For instance, Tiger Woods doesn't need to be as strong as an Olympic weightlifter to hit a golf ball; he just needs to be able to drive a golf ball. There is no hard science to suggest how strong someone needs to be, but there are some statistics available on strength requirements for particular sports. However, everyone is different and completing a biomotor ability analysis will give a good indication of how much you should focus on strength improvement.

The development of strength requires careful selection of the exercise variables (see page 124). If you are an endurance athlete, an increase in muscular endurance is better developed in sport-specific environments, whereas strength development is best achieved in the gym. Most of the strength exercises selected in this section could be considered "traditional" exercises for developing maximal strength. Be aware that for your sport you need to consider which Primal Pattern® Movements are required, and from which positions. For instance, a mixed martial artist, wrestler, or rugby player will be required to push opponents off them from the floor, so the bench press will have much carry-over into their sport. The chin-up exercise is a great exercise for the pull pattern of a rock climber or swimmer, as their sports require closed-chain pulling. If you require a pull pattern in an open-chain environment, then use a cable pull exercise (see pages 67–71) with the appropriate load.

Power

Power = work (mass x distance) ÷ time. In simple terms, power is the ability to move a mass quickly. The force velocity curve is something that is often discussed in the field of strength and conditioning. It highlights the inverse relationship between maximal force and maximal velocity. It simply means that when you are lifting close to your maximum weight, the speed of the movement is very slow. Inversely, if you move at your maximal speed, the load must be minimal. Therefore, to improve power you must not only develop strength; you must also train at fast speeds. If you have a strong, slow athlete or a weak, fast athlete, neither would be able to generate much force, especially against a load.

Terms such as "speed strength" (force developed at high velocities) or "explosive strength" (the ability to exert maximal forces in minimal time) are often used, but can be a little confusing as they are really definitions of power.

Power is also required for agility and plyometrics, which are discussed in the following sections. Many of the qualities required for power, agility, plyometrics, and speed are the same.

STARTING POSITION
- Lift the barbell from the squat rack or power rack. The bar should rest below the level of the C7 vertebra on the upper trapezius muscle.
- Slowly and carefully take three or four backward steps away from the squat rack.
- Stand with feet shoulder-width apart.

Rectus femoris

Vastus lateralis

Gluteus medius

Vastus intermedius

Gluteus maximus

Femur

Gastrocnemius

Biceps femoris

Soleus

Basic description:
- Inhale, gently drawing the navel toward the spine.
- Take a large step forward and lower the body weight down to the ground, under control.
- Allow the knees to bend and finish with the back knee about one inch from the floor.
- Keep most of the weight on the front leg.
- At the bottom of the lunge, drive straight back up to the starting position by driving the front heel through the floor, exhaling through pursed lips as you pass through the most difficult part of the ascent.

Tips for good form:
- Keep your torso upright, gently squeeze your shoulder blades together, and keep your head level with the horizon.
- Keep the front knee in line with the second toe as you descend and ascend. Do not allow the foot, ankle, or knee to move toward the mid-line.
- Keep your weight on the mid- to rear portion of your front foot.

ANALYSIS OF MOVEMENT	JOINTS	JOINT MOVEMENT	MOBILIZING MUSCLES
Joint 1	Hip	Down: flexion, Up: extension	Front leg: Gluteus maximus, gluteus medius (posterior fibers), biceps femoris, semitendinosus, semimembranosus, adductor magnus (posterior fibers)
Joint 2	Knee	Down: flexion Up: extension	Front leg: Rectus femoris, vastus medialis, vastus intermedius, vastus lateralis
Joint 3	Ankle	Down: dorsiflexion Up: plantarflexion	Front leg: Gastrocnemius, soleus, tibialis posterior, peroneus longus and brevis

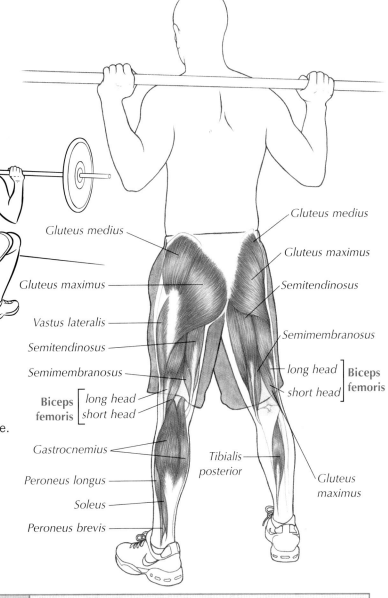

FINISH POSITION
- At the bottom of the squat, drive your heels through the floor to push yourself back up.
- Exhale through the most challenging part of the ascent.

Basic description:
- Lift the barbell from the squat rack or power rack. The bar should rest below the level of the C7 vertebra on the upper trapezius muscle.
- Slowly and carefully take two to three small backward steps away from the squat rack.
- Stand with torso upright and eyes looking straight ahead.
- Feet should be shoulder-width apart or slightly wider and can be turned out up to 30°.
- Inhale, gently drawing the navel in toward the spine.
- Descend into a squat position, as if sitting in a chair, as far as you can without your lumbar spine rounding (flexing).

Tips for good form:
- Keep the torso upright, looking straight ahead.
- Keep the knees in line with the second toe on each foot.

Gluteus medius
Gluteus maximus
Vastus lateralis
Semitendinosus
Semimembranosus
Biceps femoris [long head / short head]
Gastrocnemius
Peroneus longus
Soleus
Peroneus brevis

Gluteus medius
Gluteus maximus
Semitendinosus
Semimembranosus
long head / short head **Biceps femoris**
Tibialis posterior
Gluteus maximus

ANALYSIS OF MOVEMENT	JOINTS	JOINT MOVEMENT	MOBILIZING MUSCLES
Joint 1	Hip	Up: extension Down: flexion	Gluteus maximus, gluteus medius (posterior fibers), biceps femoris, semitendinosus, semimembranosus, adductor magnus (posterior fibers)
Joint 2	Knee	Up: extension Down: flexion	Rectus femoris, vastus medialis, vastus intermedius, vastus lateralis
Joint 3	Ankle	Up: plantarflexion Down: dorsiflexion	Gastrocnemius, soleus, tibialis posterior, peroneus longus and brevis

Basic description:

- Inhale, drawing the navel toward the spine.
- Drive the feet through the floor to initiate the ascent, exhaling through pursed lips through the most challenging part of the lift. Keep the torso at the same angle until the bar passes the knees.
- Keep the bar as close to the body as possible as you lift.
- As soon as the weight passes the knees, drive the hips forward until you are standing upright. Keep the arms straight throughout.
- At the top of the exercise, keep the navel drawn in and inhale. Then descend the weight, keeping it close to the body by bending at the hips until the weight reaches your knees, then bend the knees until the weight reaches the floor.
- Exhale through the most challenging part of the ascent and the descent.

Tips for good form:

- Ensure that the lumbar spine does not flex. If you have to, you can tape your lumbar spine with athletic tape so that you know when your spine is flexing.
- Keep the torso upright and gently draw the shoulder blades together.
- Keep your eyes level with the horizon.

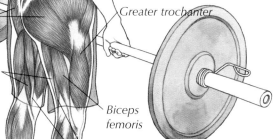

STARTING POSITION
- You should be in a bent-forward position with a barbell in front of you, feet shoulder-width apart.
- Grab the bar outside your legs and keep your spine in good alignment, with the torso facing forward.

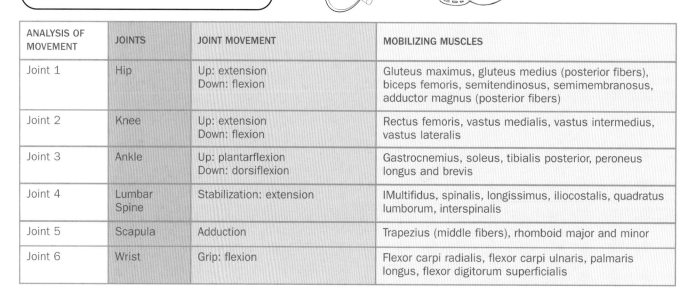

ANALYSIS OF MOVEMENT	JOINTS	JOINT MOVEMENT	MOBILIZING MUSCLES
Joint 1	Hip	Up: extension Down: flexion	Gluteus maximus, gluteus medius (posterior fibers), biceps femoris, semitendinosus, semimembranosus, adductor magnus (posterior fibers)
Joint 2	Knee	Up: extension Down: flexion	Rectus femoris, vastus medialis, vastus intermedius, vastus lateralis
Joint 3	Ankle	Up: plantarflexion Down: dorsiflexion	Gastrocnemius, soleus, tibialis posterior, peroneus longus and brevis
Joint 4	Lumbar Spine	Stabilization: extension	IMultifidus, spinalis, longissimus, iliocostalis, quadratus lumborum, interspinalis
Joint 5	Scapula	Adduction	Trapezius (middle fibers), rhomboid major and minor
Joint 6	Wrist	Grip: flexion	Flexor carpi radialis, flexor carpi ulnaris, palmaris longus, flexor digitorum superficialis

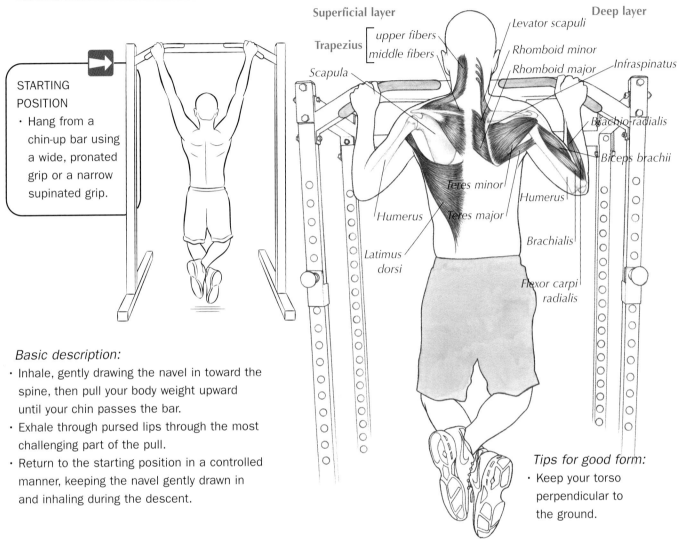

STARTING POSITION
- Hang from a chin-up bar using a wide, pronated grip or a narrow supinated grip.

Superficial layer

Deep layer

Trapezius [upper fibers / middle fibers]

Levator scapuli

Rhomboid minor

Rhomboid major

Infraspinatus

Scapula

Brachio-radialis

Biceps brachii

Teres minor

Humerus

Humerus

Teres major

Brachialis

Latimus dorsi

Flexor carpi radialis

Basic description:
- Inhale, gently drawing the navel in toward the spine, then pull your body weight upward until your chin passes the bar.
- Exhale through pursed lips through the most challenging part of the pull.
- Return to the starting position in a controlled manner, keeping the navel gently drawn in and inhaling during the descent.

Tips for good form:
- Keep your torso perpendicular to the ground.

ANALYSIS OF MOVEMENT	JOINTS	JOINT MOVEMENT	MOBILIZING MUSCLES
Joint 1	Scapula	Pulling up: downward rotation, adduction and depression Lowering: upward rotation, abduction and elevation	Levator scapula, rhomboid major and minor, trapezius (upper and middle fibers)
Joint 2	Shoulder	Pulling up: adduction Lowering: abduction	Latissimus dorsi, teres major, infraspinatus, teres minor, pectoralis major, triceps brachii (long head), coracobrachialis
Joint 3	Elbow	Pulling up: flexion Lowering: extension	Biceps brachii, brachialis, brachioradialis, flexor carpi radialis, palmaris
Joint 4	Wrist	Gripping of the bar	Flexor carpi radialis, flexor carpi ulnaris, palmaris longus, flexor digitorum superficialis

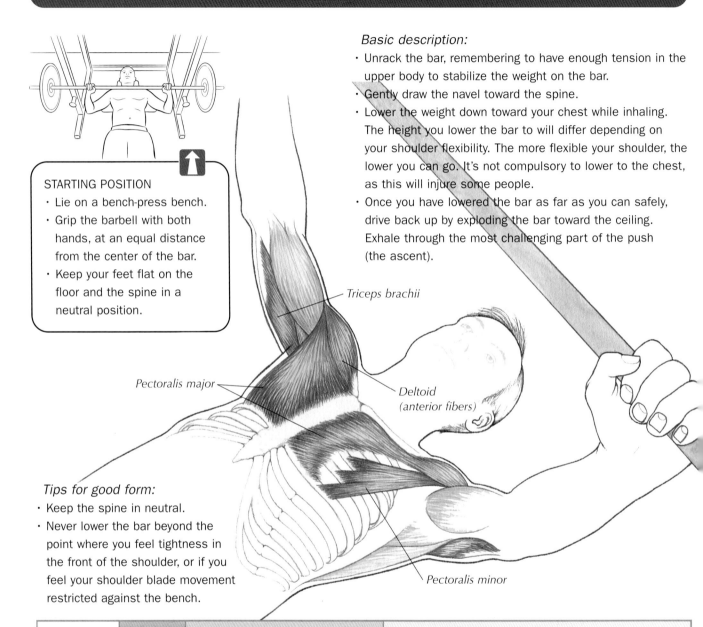

STARTING POSITION
- Lie on a bench-press bench.
- Grip the barbell with both hands, at an equal distance from the center of the bar.
- Keep your feet flat on the floor and the spine in a neutral position.

Basic description:
- Unrack the bar, remembering to have enough tension in the upper body to stabilize the weight on the bar.
- Gently draw the navel toward the spine.
- Lower the weight down toward your chest while inhaling. The height you lower the bar to will differ depending on your shoulder flexibility. The more flexible your shoulder, the lower you can go. It's not compulsory to lower to the chest, as this will injure some people.
- Once you have lowered the bar as far as you can safely, drive back up by exploding the bar toward the ceiling. Exhale through the most challenging part of the push (the ascent).

Triceps brachii

Pectoralis major

Deltoid (anterior fibers)

Pectoralis minor

Tips for good form:
- Keep the spine in neutral.
- Never lower the bar beyond the point where you feel tightness in the front of the shoulder, or if you feel your shoulder blade movement restricted against the bench.

ANALYSIS OF MOVEMENT	JOINTS	JOINT MOVEMENT	MOBILIZING MUSCLES
Joint 1	Scapula	Pushing up: abduction Lowering: adduction	Pectoralis minor, serratus anterior
Joint 2	Shoulder	Pushing up: horizontal adduction Lowering: horizontal abduction	Deltoid (anterior fibers), pectoralis major (upper fibers)
Joint 3	Elbow	Pushing up: flexion Lowering: extension	Triceps brachii, anconeus

STARTING POSITION
- Stand facing away from a cable machine. Grab the cable handle with the closest hand, with the other hand on top.
- Squat down into a half-squat position with the cable next to the nearest hip.

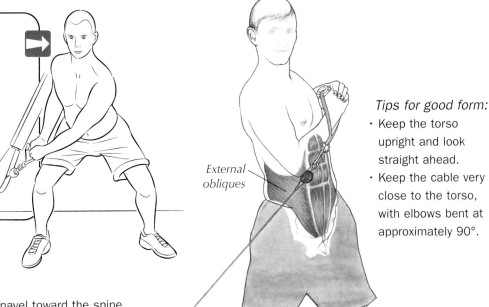

External obliques

Tips for good form:
- Keep the torso upright and look straight ahead.
- Keep the cable very close to the torso, with elbows bent at approximately 90°.

Basic description:
- Inhale and gently draw the navel toward the spine.
- Drive up to a standing position while simultaneously rotating the torso away from the cable. The cable finishes by the opposite shoulder (like throwing an upper-cut punch). Exhale through pursed lips as you move through the most challenging part of the lift.
- From the top position return back to the start, keeping the navel drawn in toward the spine. Inhale as you return back to the starting position.

ANALYSIS OF MOVEMENT	JOINTS	JOINT MOVEMENT	MOBILIZING MUSCLES
Joint 1	Ankle	Up: plantarflexion Down: dorsiflexion	Gastrocnemius, soleus, tibialis posterior, peroneus longus and brevis)
Joint 2	Knee	Up: extension Down: flexion	Rectus femoris, vastus medialis, vastus intermedius, vastus lateralis
Joint 3	Hip	Inside leg going up: extension, external rotation Outside leg going up: extension, internal rotation	Inside leg: Gluteus maximus, gluteus medius (posterior fibers), biceps femoris, semitendinosus, semimembranosus, adductor magnus (posterior fibers), biceps femoris, sartorius, psoas, iliacus, piriformis, quadratus femoris, gemellus superior and inferior, obturator externus and internus Outside leg: Gluteus maximus, gluteus medius (posterior fibers), biceps femoris, semitendinosus, semimembranosus, adductor magnus (posterior fibers), pectineus, adductor brevis, longus and magnus, gracilis, tensor fascia lata, semitendinosus, semimembranosus
Joint 4	Spine	Rotation	Ipsilateral: Internal oblique Contralateral: Multifidus, rotatores, external oblique

Basic description:

· Jump as high as possible, switching the position of the legs mid-air. Lift the medicine ball from the starting position to just outside the opposite knee on landing.

· Land in the lunge position with the opposite leg forward. On contact with the ground jump back up as quickly as possible, aiming to jump as high as you can.

Tips for good form:

· Keep the torso upright and ensure that the knees stay in line with the second toe on landing and take-off. Breathe through pursed lips as required.

STARTING POSITION
· Begin in a lunge position, with your torso upright. Hold a medicine ball (approximately 5 percent of body weight) to one side of your body.

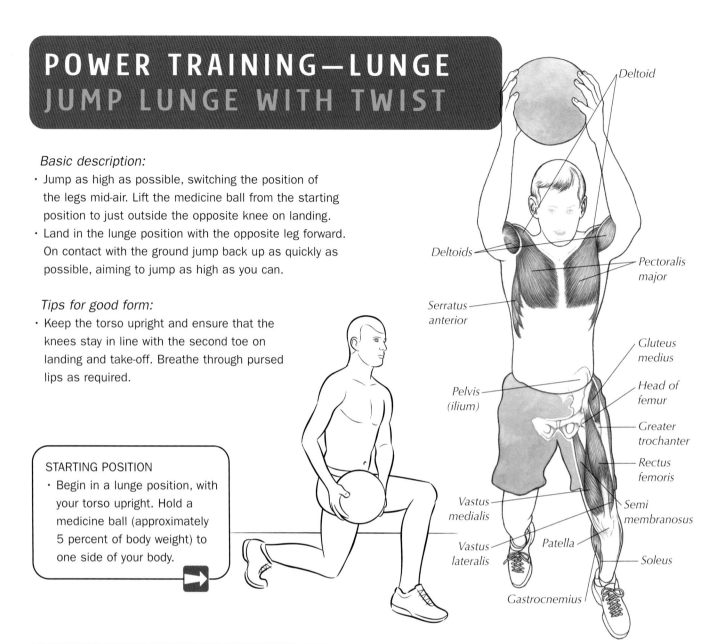

Deltoid

Deltoids

Pectoralis major

Serratus anterior

Gluteus medius

Head of femur

Pelvis (ilium)

Greater trochanter

Rectus femoris

Vastus medialis

Semi membranosus

Vastus lateralis

Patella

Soleus

Gastrocnemius

ANALYSIS OF MOVEMENT	JOINTS	JOINT MOVEMENT	MOBILIZING MUSCLES
Joint 1	Shoulder	Abduction, flexion, extension, horizontal adduction, horizontal abduction	Deltoid, supraspinatus, pectoralis major (upper fibers), biceps brachii, infraspinatus, teres minor
Joint 2	Scapulothoracic	Upward rotation, abduction, downward rotation, adduction, elevation, depression	Trapezius, levator scapula, rhomboid major and minor, pectoralis minor, serratus anterior
Joint 3	Hip	Flexion, extension	Front leg: Gluteus maximus, gluteus medius (posterior fibers), biceps femoris, semitendinosus, semimembranosus, adductor magnus (posterior fibers)
Joint 4	Knee	Flexion, extension.	Front leg: Rectus femoris, vastus medialis, vastus intermedius, vastus lateralis
Joint 5	Ankle	Plantarflexion, dorsiflexion	Gastrocnemius, soleus, tibialis posterior, peroneus longus and brevis

POWER TRAINING—SQUAT
JUMP SQUAT

Tips for good form:
- Ensure you achieve triple extension—of the hips, knees, and ankles (plantarflexion).
- Don't drop into a full squat before completing the succeeding jump squat.

STARTING POSITION
- Stand upright with feet approximately hip-width apart. If wanted, you can use a medicine ball (approximately 10 percent of body weight) held against the chest.

Basic description:
- Drop down into a half-squat position, then explode upward, driving the feet through the floor, gaining as much height as possible.
- On landing, keep the contact time as short as possible.
- You can use your arms to help create lift, depending on whether it is functional for your sport.

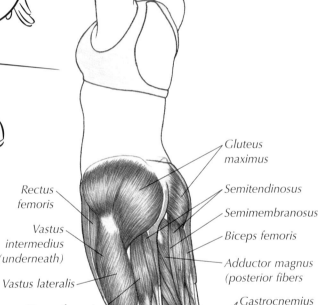

Gluteus maximus

Rectus femoris

Semitendinosus

Semimembranosus

Vastus intermedius (underneath)

Biceps femoris

Vastus lateralis

Adductor magnus (posterior fibers)

Biceps femoris

Gastrocnemius

Soleus

Peroneus longus

Peroneus brevis

ANALYSIS OF MOVEMENT	JOINTS	JOINT MOVEMENT	MOBILIZING MUSCLES
Joint 1	Hip	Down: flexion Up: extension	Gluteus maximus, gluteus medius (posterior fibers), biceps femoris, semitendinosus, semimembranosus, adductor magnus (posterior fibers)
Joint 2	Knee	Down: flexion Up: extension	Rectus femoris, vastus medialis, vastus intermedius, vastus lateralis
Joint 3	Ankle	Down: dorsiflexion Up: plantarflexion	Gastrocnemius, soleus, tibialis posterior, peroneus longus and brevis

POWER TRAINING—BEND
POWER CLEAN

Basic description:
- Inhale, drawing the navel toward the spine.
- Drive the feet through the floor to initiate the ascent, exhaling through pursed lips through the most challenging part of the lift. Keep the torso at the same angle until the weight passes the knees.
- Keep the weight as close to the body as possible as you lift.
- As soon as the weight passes the knees, drive the hips forward as you perform triple extension and pull the bar upward explosively. As the bar reaches the lower chest region, drop under the bar, catching it on the shoulders with elbows up high.
- Return the weight to the floor, keeping it close to the body.

Tips for good form:
- Ensure that the lumbar spine does not flex. If you have to, you can tape your lumbar spine with athletic tape so you know when your spine is flexing.
- Keep the torso upright and gently draw the shoulder blades together.
- Keep your eyes level with the horizon.

STARTING POSITION
- Begin in a bent forward position with a barbell in front of you, feet shoulder-width apart
- Grab the bar outside your legs and keep the spine in good alignment, with the torso facing forward.

ANALYSIS OF MOVEMENT	JOINTS	JOINT MOVEMENT	MOBILIZING MUSCLES
Joint 1	Hip	Up: extension Down: flexion	Gluteus maximus, gluteus medius (posterior fibers), biceps femoris, semitendinosus, semimembranosus, adductor magnus (posterior fibers)
Joint 2	Knee	Up: extension Down: flexion	Rectus femoris, vastus medialis, vastus intermedius, vastus lateralis
Joint 3	Ankle	Up: plantarflexion Down: dorsiflexion	Gastrocnemius, soleus, tibialis posterior, peroneus longus and brevis
Joint 4	Lumbar spine	Stabilization: extension	Multifidus, spinalis, longissimus, iliocostalis, quadratus lumborum, interspinalis
Joint 5	Scapula	Adduction, elevation, upward rotation	Trapezius, rhomboid major and minor
Joint 6	Shoulder	Flexion, external rotation	Deltoid (anterior fibers), pectoralis major (upper fibers), infraspinatus, teres minor
Joint 7	Wrist	Grip: flexion Catch: extension	Grip: Flexor carpi radialis, flexor carpi ulnaris, palmaris longus, flexor digitorum superficialis Catch: Extensor carpi radialis longus and brevis, extensor carpi ulnaris

POWER TRAINING—PULL
INVERTED BAR PULL

Tips for good form:
· Keep the navel drawn gently in.

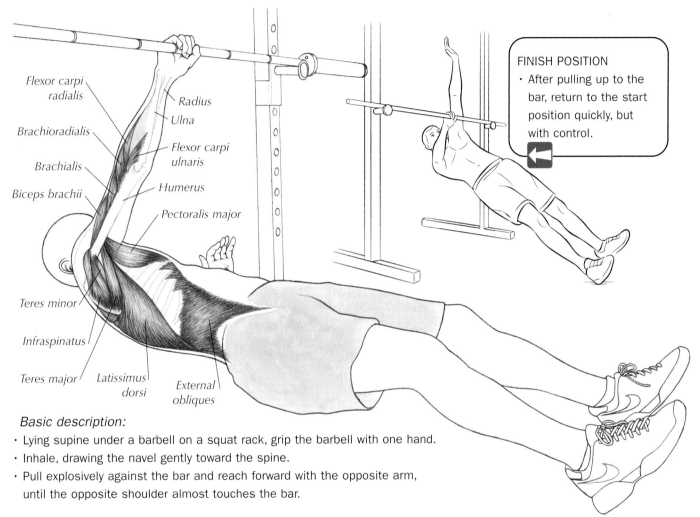

Flexor carpi radialis

Radius

Ulna

Brachioradialis

Flexor carpi ulnaris

Brachialis

Humerus

Biceps brachii

Pectoralis major

Teres minor

Infraspinatus

Teres major

Latissimus dorsi

External obliques

FINISH POSITION
· After pulling up to the bar, return to the start position quickly, but with control.

Basic description:
· Lying supine under a barbell on a squat rack, grip the barbell with one hand.
· Inhale, drawing the navel gently toward the spine.
· Pull explosively against the bar and reach forward with the opposite arm, until the opposite shoulder almost touches the bar.

ANALYSIS OF MOVEMENT	JOINTS	JOINT MOVEMENT	MOBILIZING MUSCLES
Joint 1	Scapula	Pulling up: downward rotation, adduction, and depression. Lowering: upward rotation, abduction, and elevation	Levator scapula, rhomboid major and minor, trapezius (middle and lower fibers)
Joint 2	Shoulder	Pulling up: adduction Lowering: abduction	Latissimus dorsi, teres major, infraspinatus, teres minor, pectoralis major, triceps brachii (long head), coracobrachialis
Joint 3	Elbow	Pulling up: flexion Lowering: extension	Biceps brachii, brachialis, brachioradialis, flexor carpi radialis, palmaris
Joint 4	Wrist	Gripping the bar	Flexor carpi radialis, flexor carpi ulnaris, palmaris longus, flexor digitorum superficialis
Joint 5	Spine	Rotation	Contralateral: Internal oblique Ipsilateral: Multifidus, rotatores, external oblique

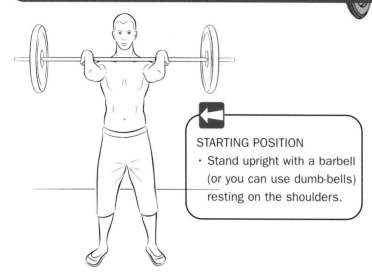

STARTING POSITION
- Stand upright with a barbell (or you can use dumb-bells) resting on the shoulders.

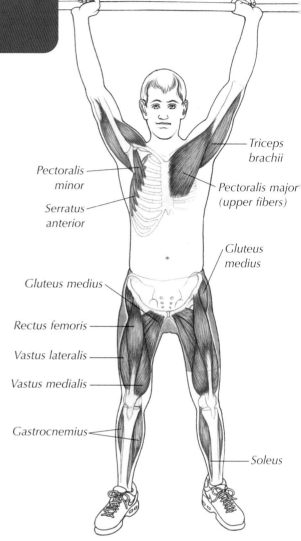

Triceps brachii

Pectoralis minor

Serratus anterior

Pectoralis major (upper fibers)

Gluteus medius

Gluteus medius

Rectus femoris

Vastus lateralis

Vastus medialis

Gastrocnemius

Soleus

Basic description:
- Inhale, gently drawing the navel toward the spine.
- Descend into a half-squat, then drive up explosively, using triple extension to drive the bar overhead. As the bar moves overhead, drop quickly under it into a solid lunge or half-squat position.
- Return the bar slowly to the shoulders.

Tips for good form:
- Lock out the elbows with the bar overhead.
- Ensure that the knees are straight in line with the second toe of the foot on landing.

ANALYSIS OF MOVEMENT	JOINTS	JOINT MOVEMENT	MOBILIZING MUSCLES
Joint 1	Scapula	Pushing up: abduction. Lowering: adduction	Pectoralis minor, serratus anterior
Joint 2	Shoulder	Pushing up: horizontal adduction Lowering: horizontal abduction	Deltoid (anterior fibers), pectoralis major (upper fibers)
Joint 3	Elbow	Pushing up: flexion Lowering: extension	Triceps brachii, anconeus
Joint 4	Hip	Dip down: flexion Drive up: extension	Gluteus maximus, gluteus medius (posterior fibers), biceps femoris, semitendinosus, semimembranosus, adductor magnus (posterior fibers)
Joint 5	Knee	Dip down: flexion Drive up: extension	Rectus femoris, vastus medialis, vastus intermedius, vastus lateralis
Joint 6	Ankle	Dip down: dorsiflexion Drive up: plantarflexion	Gastrocnemius, soleus, tibialis posterior, peroneus longus and brevis

POWER TRAINING—TWIST
MEDICINE BALL SIDE TOSS

Tips for good form:
· Maintain an upright torso, with your
  eyes following the medicine ball.
· Maintain a slight bend in
  the elbows.
· Shift your body weight sideways,
  rotate the torso, then express the
  twist with the arms by releasing
  the ball.

Basic description:
· Inhale, gently drawing your navel
  toward your spine.
· Push off the foot farthest from the
  wall, driving your body weight
  toward it. Rotate the torso and release the ball
  toward the wall with as much force as possible.
· Catch the ball on its return from the wall while
  returning to the starting position.
· Complete the next repetition as soon as
  you reach the starting position again.

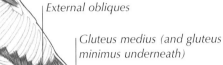

STARTING POSITION
· Stand side-on to a solid wall holding a
  medicine ball (5–10 percent of body weight).
· Allow 70 percent of your weight to be
  supported by the leg farthest from the
  wall, with the medicine ball held over
  the farthest knee from the wall, with
  arms almost straight.

Deltoid
Humerus
Teres minor
Infraspinatus
Internal
obliques
Pelvis
Vastus intermedius
Sartorius
Rectus femoris
Vastus
medialis

External obliques
Gluteus medius (and gluteus
minimus underneath)
Tensor fascia latae
Sartorius
Pectineus
Adductor brevis,
longus and
magnus
Gracilis
Adductors
Biceps femoris
Gastrocnemius
Soleus

ANALYSIS OF MOVEMENT	JOINTS	JOINT MOVEMENT	MOBILIZING MUSCLES
Joint 1	Spine	Rotation	Ipsilateral: Internal oblique Contralateral: Multifidus, rotatores, external oblique
Joint 2	Scapula	Abduction, adduction,	Outside arm: Pectoralis minor, serratus anterior Inside arm: Trapezius (middle fibers), rhomboid major and minor
Joint 3	Shoulder	Horizontal adduction, horizontal abduction	Outside arm: Deltoid (anterior fibers), pectoralis major (upper fibers) Inside arm: Deltoid (posterior fibers), infraspinatus, teres minor
Joint 4	Hip	Internal rotation, lateral rotation, abduction, adduction, extension, flexion	Outside leg: Gluteus maximus, gluteus medius (posterior fibers), biceps femoris, semitendinosus, semimembranosus, adductor magnus (posterior fibers), sartorius, psoas, iliacus, piriformis, quadratus femoris, gemellus superior and inferior, obturator externus and internus Inside leg: Gluteus maximus, gluteus medius, gluteus minimus, tensor fascia lata, sartorius, pectineus, adductor brevis, longus and magnus, gracilis, tensor fascia lata, semitendinosus, semimembranosus
Joint 5	Knee	Extension, flexion	Outside leg: Rectus femoris, vastus medialis, vastus intermedius, vastus lateralis
Joint 6	Ankle	Plantarflexion, dorsiflexion	Outside leg: Gastrocnemius, soleus, tibialis posterior, peroneus longus and brevis
Joint 7	Foot	Eversion	Outside leg: Peroneus longus and brevis, extensor digitorum longus

AGILITY

In the first section of this book, I suggested that agility is "a speedy change of direction involving a deceleration, followed by an acceleration in response to a stimulus in any direction while maintaining balance." This stimulus refers to a visual, audio, or physical inducement.

Agility has also been described as "the ability to explosively start, decelerate, change direction, and accelerate quickly again while maintaining body control and minimizing loss of speed" (D. Chu, *Jumping Into Plyometrics*). The key to agility is to minimize loss of speed while moving the body's center of gravity under control.

The drills in this section can help you to change direction quickly and efficiently whether forward, backward, upward, sideway, or rotation. Agility requires good eccentric and concentric strength, speed, power, balance, flexibility, and co-ordination. A strong correlation has been found to exist between lower body strength and agility. Therefore, your biomotor ability profile (see page 127) is crucial to highlight the qualities you need in order to ensure that you can develop optimal agility.

It has often been suggested that agility is a primary indicator of success in sport. So why is agility so vital to performance? When you look at racket sports and field sports, such as soccer, rugby, and field hockey, it becomes very apparent. Tennis rallies generally last between 2.7 and 10.7 seconds, badminton rallies last between 6 and 9 seconds, and squash rallies last on average approximately 15 seconds. The small size of the courts means that these sports require constant movements toward the ball (or shuttle), with a return to a central position between each shot, with multiple shots per rally, and therefore many changes of direction at speed.

Field sports typically involve sprints of 33–66 ft (10–20 m), every one to two minutes and some 20–60 times per game. These sprints can include changes of direction, jumping, cutting, and quick deceleration, often requiring a high level of skill during or at the end of the sprint. It has also been shown that there is a "direct correlation between increased agility and development of athletic timing, rhythm, and movement" (D. Chu, *Jumping Into Plyometrics*).

Agility training

So how do you improve agility? The agility drills in this section enable important neural adaptations that require many repetitions over time to achieve improvement. Some experts suggest that to improve agility for your sport, you need to train in your sport rather than in drills. However, the advantage to practicing agility drills in a non-competitive environment is that you are able to receive immediate feedback from a coach, or yourself if you have a video recorder. This way, faulty technique can be corrected quickly and efficiently through repetitive practice. As Chek states, "perfect practice makes perfect" (*Movement That Matters*).

The list of agility drills in this section is by no means a finite list. You should use the drills that are similar to the movements in your sport—or use the drills to spark ideas and design drills that are similar to your sport. In general terms, each set should take around 5 to 10 seconds. The work/rest ratio should be 1:3 or 1:4 for optimal gains.

When practicing drills, there are a few general technique tips to focus on. The wider the base of support and the lower the center of mass, the more stability you have, and the more you are able to decelerate efficiently. The opposite is required to create acceleration. In other words, the base of support is reduced and the center of mass is higher. The arms should also be used to generate rotational force or counter-rotation when changing direction. When decelerating, body weight should not lean backward.

As you improve your agility, you also need to consider that your opponents' movements can affect your movement decision-making. Drills can be progressed to include reaction speed and decision-making, either by a coach or a training partner. You can also add a skill element of your sport when you reach an advanced stage of agility development.

AGILITY DRILLS

HEXAGON DRILL

Basic description:
· On two feet, jump outside the hexagon forward and then back to the center.
· Repeat by jumping outside each line in the hexagon and back to the middle as quickly as possible in a clockwise direction. Complete at least once around all six sides of the hexagon.
· Repeat in an anti-clockwise direction.

ANALYSIS OF MOVEMENT	JOINTS	JOINT MOVEMENT	MOBILIZING MUSCLES
Joint 1	Hip	Extension, flexion, internal rotation, lateral rotation, abduction, adduction	Gluteus maximus, gluteus medius, gluteus minimus, biceps femoris, sartorius, psoas, iliacus, piriformis, quadratus femoris, gemellus superior and inferior, obturator externus and internus, tensor fascia lata, pectineus, adductor brevis, longus and magnus, gracilis, semitendinosus, semimembranosus
Joint 2	Knee	Extension, flexion	Rectus femoris, vastus medialis, vastus intermedius, vastus lateralis
Joint 3	Ankle	Plantarflexion, dorsiflexion	Gastrocnemius, soleus, tibialis posterior, peroneus longus and brevis
Joint 4	Foot	Eversion, inversion	Peroneus longus and brevis, extensor digitorum longus, tibialis anterior and posterior, flexor digitorum longus, flexor hallucis longus, extensor hallucis longus

STARTING POSITION
· Stand inside a marked hexagon on the floor, with sides 24 in (60 cm) long.

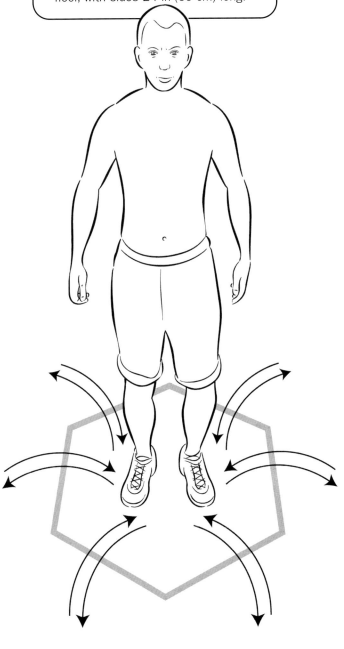

Tips for good form:
· Keep the head and torso up.
· Stay on the balls of your feet and keep the ground contact as short as possible.

180° TURN LADDER DRILL

Basic description:

- Jump and rotate 180° so you land with your feet astride the first rung of the ladder, facing the opposite way.
- On landing, jump immediately, rotating 180° again to land astride the second rung, facing the same way as you started. Continue to the end of the ladder.

Tips for good form:

- Keep the head and torso up.
- Stay on the balls of your feet and keep the ground contact as short as possible.

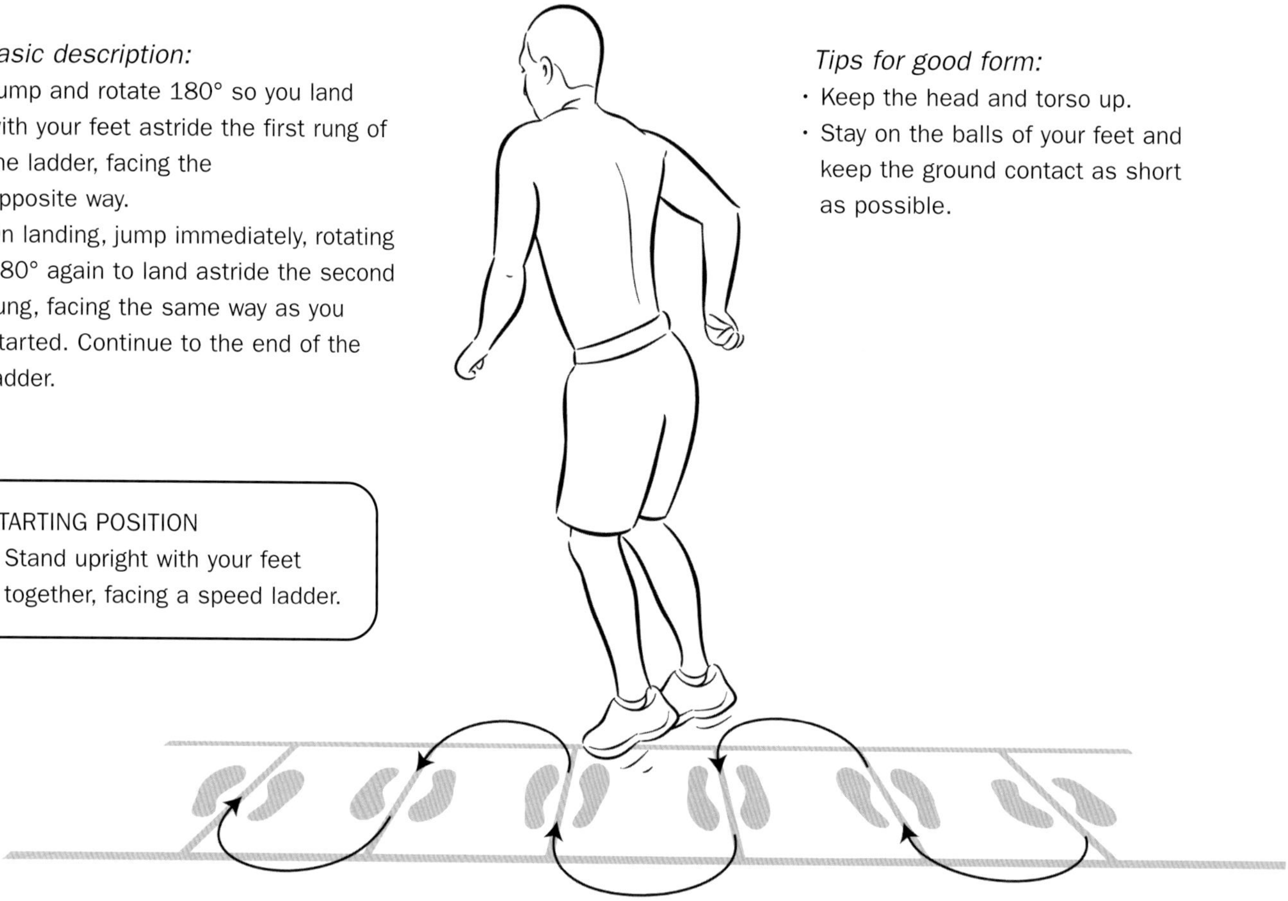

STARTING POSITION
- Stand upright with your feet together, facing a speed ladder.

ANALYSIS OF MOVEMENT	JOINTS	JOINT MOVEMENT	MOBILIZING MUSCLES
Joint 1	Shoulder	Extension, flexion	Deltoid (anterior & posterior fibers), latissimus dorsi, teres major, infraspinatus, teres minor, pectoralis major, triceps brachii (long head), biceps brachii
Joint 2	Scapula	Upward rotation, downward rotation, abduction, adduction	Trapezius, pectoralis minor, serratus anterior, levator scapula, rhomboid major and minor
Joint 3	Spine	Rotation	Ipsilateral: Internal oblique Contralateral: Multifidus, rotatores, external oblique.
Joint 4	Hip	Extension, flexion, internal rotation, lateral rotation	Gluteus maximus, gluteus medius, gluteus minimus, biceps femoris, sartorius, psoas, iliacus, piriformis, quadratus femoris, gemellus superior and inferior, obturator externus and internus, tensor fascia lata, pectineus, adductor brevis, longus and magnus, gracilis, semitendinosus, semimembranosus
Joint 5	Knee	Extension, flexion	Rectus femoris, vastus medialis, vastus intermedius, vastus lateralis
Joint 6	Ankle	Plantarflexion, dorsiflexion	Gastrocnemius, soleus, tibialis posterior, peroneus longus and brevis

ZIG-ZAG CROSSOVER SHUFFLE LADDER DRILL

STARTING POSITION
· Stand with your feet hip-width apart to the left of the first rung of a speed ladder.

Basic description:
· Cross over your left foot into the first square of the ladder (1).
· Take your right leg behind your left leg to the right side of the first square (2).
· Step with your left leg to just outside the first square to the right, to join your right leg (3).
· Crossover your right leg in front of the left leg and into the second square of the ladder (4).
· The left leg then goes behind the right leg to the left side of the second square (5).
· The right leg then steps laterally to just outside the second square on the left side, to join the left leg (6).
· Continue this pattern all the way along the ladder (7–9).
· Repeat by starting on the right of the ladder.

Tips for good form:
· Use a light and quick foot strike.
· Begin slowly, build good technique, and foot placement accuracy. Then, increase speed. Avoid landing on the rungs of the ladder.
· Keep looking straight ahead with your torso up once you've mastered the steps.

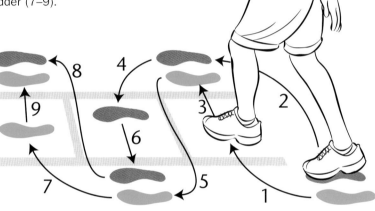

ANALYSIS OF MOVEMENT	JOINTS	JOINT MOVEMENT	MOBILIZING MUSCLES
Joint 1	Shoulder	Flexion, extension, internal rotation, external rotation, horizontal adduction, horizontal abduction	Deltoid (anterior and posterior fibers), pectoralis major, biceps brachii, latissimus dorsi, teres major, infraspinatus, teres minor, triceps brachii (long head), subscapularis
Joint 2	Scapula	Upward rotation, downward rotation, abduction, adduction	Trapezius, pectoralis minor, serratus anterior, levator scapula, rhomboid major and minor
Joint 3	Spine	Rotation	Ipsilateral: Internal oblique Contralateral: Multifidus, rotatores, external oblique
Joint 4	Hip	Extension, flexion, internal rotation, lateral rotation, abduction, adduction	Gluteus maximus, gluteus medius, biceps femoris, semitendinosus, semimembranosus, psoas, iliacus, rectus femoris, tensor fascia lata, sartorius, adductor brevis, longus and magnus, gluteus minimus, pectineus, gracilis, piriformis, quadratus femoris, gemellus superior and inferior, obturator externus and internus
Joint 5	Knee	Extension, flexion	Rectus femoris, vastus medialis, vastus intermedius, vastus lateralis
Joint 6	Ankle	Plantarflexion, dorsiflexion, eversion, inversion	Gastrocnemius, soleus, tibialis posterior, peroneus longus and brevis, extensor digitorum longus

"A" MOVEMENT CONE DRILL

Basic description:
- Sprint to cone two.
- Shuffle sideway to cone three and back to cone two.
- Sprint forward to cone four.
- Back-pedal to cone five.
- Repeat in the opposite direction by starting at cone five.

Tips for good form:
- Drive the arms when sprinting, side-shuffling, and back-pedalling.
- Use small, fast steps to aid deceleration and prepare for direction change.
- Lean the torso slightly forward when back-pedalling.

STARTING POSITION
- Begin at cone one in the ready position.

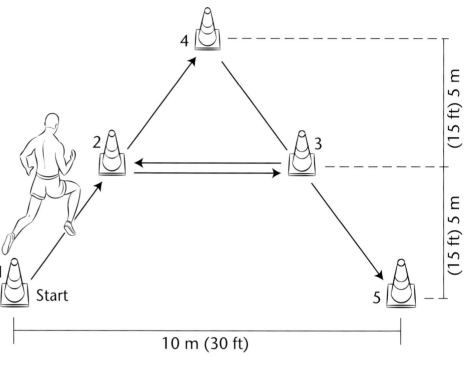

ANALYSIS OF MOVEMENT	JOINTS	JOINT MOVEMENT	MOBILIZING MUSCLES
Joint 1	Shoulder	Flexion, extension, internal rotation, external rotation, horizontal adduction	Deltoid (anterior and posterior fibers), pectoralis major, biceps brachii, latissimus dorsi, teres major, infraspinatus, teres minor, triceps brachii (long head), subscapularis
Joint 2	Scapula	Upward rotation, downward rotation, abduction, adduction	Trapezius, pectoralis minor, serratus anterior, levator scapula, rhomboid major and minor
Joint 3	Spine	Rotation	Ipsilateral: Internal oblique Contralateral: Multifidus, rotatores, external oblique
Joint 4	Hip	Extension, flexion, internal rotation, lateral rotation, abduction, adduction	Gluteus maximus, gluteus medius (posterior fibers), biceps femoris, semitendinosus, semimembranosus, psoas, iliacus, rectus femoris, tensor fascia lata, sartorius, adductor brevis, longus and magnus, gluteus medius gluteus minimus, pectineus, gracilis, piriformis, quadratus femoris, gemellus superior and inferior, obturator externus and internus
Joint 5	Knee	Extension, flexion	Rectus femoris, vastus medialis, vastus intermedius, vastus lateralis
Joint 6	Ankle	Plantarflexion, dorsiflexion, eversion, inversion	Gastrocnemius, soleus, tibialis posterior, peroneus longus and brevis, extensor digitorum longus

"Z" PATTERN RUN CONE DRILL

Tips for good form:
- Use small, fast steps to aid deceleration and prepare for direction change.
- Plant the outside foot and drive off it to change direction.
- Drive the arms to aid acceleration and speed.

Basic description:
- Sprint diagonally 15 ft (5 m) to the closest cone and run around it.
- Change direction and sprint diagonally to the next closest cone.
- Continue this movement around all the cones.
- Repeat in the opposite direction.

STARTING POSITION
- Start at the first cone in a ready position.

(15 ft) 5 m

(15 ft) 5 m

(30 ft) 10 m

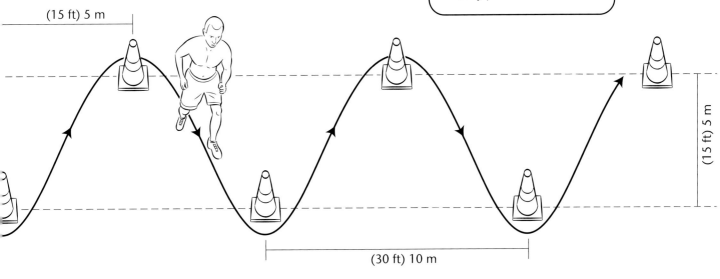

ANALYSIS OF MOVEMENT	JOINTS	JOINT MOVEMENT	MOBILIZING MUSCLES
Joint 1	Shoulder	Flexion, extension, internal rotation, external rotation, horizontal adduction, horizontal abduction	Deltoid (anterior and posterior fibers), pectoralis major, biceps brachii, latissimus dorsi, teres major, infraspinatus, teres minor, triceps brachii (long head), subscapularis
Joint 2	Scapula	Upward rotation, downward rotation, abduction, adduction	Trapezius, pectoralis minor, serratus anterior, levator scapula, rhomboid major and minor
Joint 3	Spine	Rotation	Ipsilateral: Internal oblique Contralateral: Multifidus, rotatores, external oblique
Joint 4	Hip	Extension, flexion, internal rotation, lateral rotation, abduction, adduction	Gluteus maximus, gluteus medius, biceps femoris, semitendinosus, semimembranosus, psoas, iliacus, rectus femoris, tensor fascia lata, sartorius, adductor brevis, longus and magnus, gluteus minimus, pectineus, gracilis, piriformis, quadratus femoris, gemellus superior and inferior, obturator externus and internus
Joint 5	Knee	Extension, flexion	Rectus femoris, vastus medialis, vastus intermedius, vastus lateralis
Joint 6	Ankle	Plantarflexion, dorsiflexion, eversion, inversion	Gastrocnemius, soleus, tibialis posterior, peroneus longus and brevis, extensor digitorum longus

"X" PATTERN MULTI-RUN CONE DRILL

Tips for good form:
- Use small, fast steps to aid deceleration and prepare for direction change.
- Drive the arms to aid acceleration and speed.

Basic description:
- Sprint 30 ft (10 m) to cone one.
- Change direction and sprint diagonally to cone two.
- At cone two, back-pedal to cone three.
- Sprint diagonally to cone four.
- Repeat in the opposite direction by beginning at cone two.

STARTING POSITION
- Begin in the ready position at cone four (start/finish).

3

2

1

4

Start

ANALYSIS OF MOVEMENT	JOINTS	JOINT MOVEMENT	MOBILIZING MUSCLES
Joint 1	Shoulder	Flexion, extension, internal rotation, external rotation, horizontal adduction	Deltoid (anterior and posterior fibers), pectoralis major, biceps brachii, latissimus dorsi, teres major, infraspinatus, teres minor, triceps brachii (long head), subscapularis
Joint 2	Scapula	Upward rotation, downward rotation, abduction, adduction	Trapezius, pectoralis minor, serratus anterior, levator scapula, rhomboid major and minor
Joint 3	Spine	Rotation	Ipsilateral: Internal oblique Contralateral: Multifidus, rotatores, external oblique
Joint 4	Hip	Extension, flexion, internal rotation, lateral rotation, abduction, adduction	Gluteus maximus, gluteus medius, biceps femoris, semitendinosus, semimembranosus, psoas, iliacus, rectus femoris, tensor fascia lata, sartorius, adductor brevis, longus and magnus, gluteus minimus, pectineus, gracilis, piriformis, quadratus femoris, gemellus superior and inferior, obturator externus and internus
Joint 5	Knee	Extension, flexion	Rectus femoris, vastus medialis, vastus intermedius, vastus lateralis
Joint 6	Ankle	Plantarflexion, dorsiflexion, eversion, inversion	Gastrocnemius, soleus, tibialis posterior, peroneus longus and brevis, extensor digitorum longus

SQUARE CONE DRILL

Basic description:
- Sprint 15 ft (5 m) to cone two.
- At cone two, make a sharp cut right and side-shuffle to cone three.
- At cone three, change direction and back-pedal to cone four.
- At cone four, make a sharp cut left and side-shuffle back to cone one.
- Repeat in the opposite direction by starting at cone four.

Tips for good form:
- Drive the arms to aid acceleration and speed.
- Use small, fast steps to aid deceleration and prepare for direction change.
- Plant the outside foot and drive off it to change direction.

STARTING POSITION
- Begin in the ready position at cone one (start/finish).

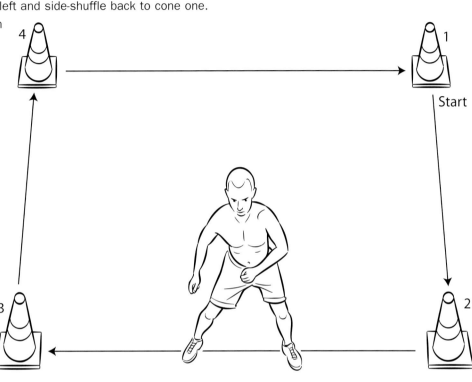

ANALYSIS OF MOVEMENT	JOINTS	JOINT MOVEMENT	MOBILIZING MUSCLES
Joint 1	Shoulder	Flexion, extension, internal rotation, external rotation, horizontal adduction, horizontal abduction	Deltoid (anterior and posterior fibers), pectoralis major, biceps brachii, latissimus dorsi, teres major, infraspinatus, teres minor, triceps brachii (long head), subscapularis
Joint 2	Scapula	Upward rotation, downward rotation, abduction, adduction	Trapezius, pectoralis minor, serratus anterior, levator scapula, rhomboid major and minor
Joint 3	Spine	Rotation	Ipsilateral: Internal oblique Contralateral: Multifidus, rotatores, external oblique
Joint 4	Hip	Extension, flexion, internal rotation, lateral rotation, abduction, adduction	Gluteus maximus, gluteus medius, biceps femoris, semitendinosus, semimembranosus, psoas, iliacus, rectus femoris, tensor fascia lata, sartorius, adductor brevis, longus and magnus, gluteus minimus, pectineus, gracilis, piriformis, quadratus femoris, gemellus superior and inferior, obturator externus and internus
Joint 5	Knee	Extension, flexion	Rectus femoris, vastus medialis, vastus intermedius, vastus lateralis
Joint 6	Ankle	Plantarflexion, dorsiflexion, eversion, inversion	Gastrocnemius, soleus, tibialis posterior, peroneus longus and brevis, extensor digitorum longus

BACK-PEDAL—FORWARD

Basic description:
- Back-pedal 15 ft (5 m) to the first set of cones (2).
- Change direction and accelerate back to the starting line (3).
- At the starting line, quickly change direction and back-pedal 30 ft (10 m) to the second set of cones (4).
- At the second set of cones, quickly accelerate and run to the starting line (5).
- At the starting line, back-pedal 15 ft (5 m) to the first set of cones (6).
- Change direction and accelerate back to the starting/finish line (7).

Tips for good form:
- Drive the arms to aid acceleration and speed.
- Use small, fast steps to aid deceleration and prepare for direction change.

STARTING POSITION
- Begin in the ready position, facing away from the cones (1).

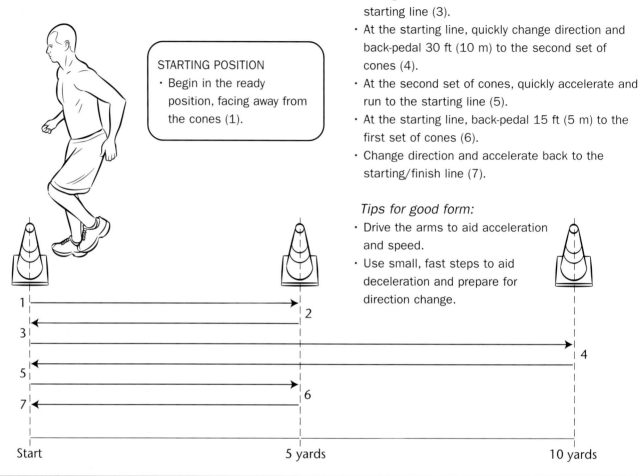

ANALYSIS OF MOVEMENT	JOINTS	JOINT MOVEMENT	MOBILIZING MUSCLES
Joint 1	Shoulder	Extension, flexion	Deltoid (anterior and posterior fibers), latissimus dorsi, teres major, infraspinatus, teres minor, pectoralis major, triceps brachii (long head), biceps brachii
Joint 2	Scapula	Upward rotation, downward rotation, abduction, adduction	Trapezius, pectoralis minor, serratus anterior, levator scapula, rhomboid major and minor
Joint 3	Spine	Rotation	Ipsilateral: Internal oblique Contralateral: Multifidus, rotatores, external oblique
Joint 4	Hip	Extension, flexion	Gluteus maximus, gluteus medius, biceps femoris, semitendinosus, semimembranosus, psoas, iliacus, rectus femoris, tensor fascia lata, sartorius, adductor brevis, longus and magnus, gluteus minimus
Joint 5	Knee	Extension, flexion	Rectus femoris, vastus medialis, vastus intermedius, vastus lateralis
Joint 6	Ankle	Plantarflexion, dorsiflexion	Gastrocnemius, soleus, tibialis posterior, peroneus longus and brevis

LATERAL SHUFFLE

Tips for good form:
- Drive the arms to aid acceleration and speed.
- Plant the outside foot and drive off it to change direction.

Basic description:
- Side-shuffle 15 ft (5 m) to the second cone (2).
- At cone two, change direction and side-shuffle back to the first cone (3).
- At cone one, change direction and side-shuffle 30 ft (10 m) to the third cone (4).
- At cone three, change direction and side-shuffle back to cone one (5).
- At cone one, change direction and side-shuffle back to cone two (6).
- At cone two, change direction and side-shuffle back to cone one (7).

STARTING POSITION
- Begin with feet shoulder-width apart at the first cone (1).

(30 ft) 10 m   (15 ft) 5 m   Start

ANALYSIS OF MOVEMENT	JOINTS	JOINT MOVEMENT	MOBILIZING MUSCLES
Joint 1	Shoulder	Extension, flexion	Deltoid (anterior and posterior fibers), latissimus dorsi, teres major, infraspinatus, teres minor, pectoralis major, triceps brachii (long head), biceps brachii
Joint 2	Scapula	Upward rotation, downward rotation, abduction, adduction	Trapezius, pectoralis minor, serratus anterior, levator scapula, rhomboid major and minor
Joint 3	Hip	Abduction, adduction	Gluteus maximus, gluteus medius, biceps femoris, semitendinosus, semimembranosus, psoas, iliacus, rectus femoris, tensor fascia lata, sartorius, adductor brevis, longus and magnus, gluteus minimus
Joint 4	Knee	Extension, flexion	Rectus femoris, vastus medialis, vastus intermedius, astus lateralis
Joint 5	Knee	Plantarflexion, dorsiflexion, eversion, inversion	Gastrocnemius, soleus, tibialis posterior, peroneus longus and brevis

"Plyometrics" was originally known as "jump training" as it mainly consisted of jumping exercises. The true interpretation of the Latin word *plyometrics* is "measurable increases."

Plyometrics is a technique that links strength with speed to produce power. "Plyometric training enables a muscle or muscle group to reach its maximum force in the shortest period of time" (H. Newton, *Explosive Lifting for Sports)*. Whether your sport involves jumping, running, throwing, or lifting, plyometric training can greatly enhance your performance.

How do plyometrics work?

Plyometrics include what is known as the "stretch-shortening cycle" (SSC). This is the loading of a muscle eccentrically, followed by rapid concentric muscle contraction. The elastic quality of muscle stores energy in the tissues during the eccentric contraction, just like stretching an elastic band. The subsequent concentric contraction uses the stored energy to contract more forcibly than it would without the prior stretch.

The stretch reflex of a muscle is activated when a muscle is lengthened very quickly. The muscle's internal receptors, known as muscle spindles, run the length of the muscle and regulate the rate of change in the length of the muscle. Upon activation of a rapid stretch, the muscle spindles send an afferent nerve impulse to the spinal cord, which then sends an efferent nerve impulse back to the muscle to contract to prevent it over-stretching and tearing. This impulse, along with the release of elastic energy as kinetic energy, produces the increased force production in the SSC.

Intensity					
High					
					Depth jumps
				Box drills	
			Multiple hops and jumps		
		Standing jumps			
	Jumps in place				
Low					
	Exercises				

Intensity scale for jump exercises, referenced from D. Chu, *Jumping Into Plyometrics*

Number of Foot Contacts by Phase of Training for Jump Training				
	Level			
	Beginner	Intermediate	Advanced	Intensity
Off-season	60–100	100–150	120–200	Low–mod
Pre-season	100–250	150–300	150–450	Mod–high
In-season	Depends on sport			Moderate
Championship season	Recovery only			Mod–high

Adapted from D. Chu, *Jumping Into Plyometrics*

The stretch reflex, or myotatic reflex as it is also known, responds to the rate at which the muscle is being stretched and is among the fastest reflexes in the body.

The conversion from eccentric to concentric work is known as the amortization phase. This phase lasts just hundredths of a second. The shorter the amortization phase, the greater the force production. The slower the amortization phase, the less power advantage you will gain from the SSC. Plyometric training enables a shorter amortization phase.

Plyometric training

It has been suggested that before taking part in plyometric training, you should be able to squat 1.5 times your body weight. In reality, most sports have plyometric movements that utilize the SSC. The table above (top) indicates the level of intensity of differing plyometric exercises. Each of the plyometric exercises in this section can be categorized as either jumps in place, standing jumps, multiple hops-and-jumps, box drills, or depth jumps. The requirements of your sport and your level of conditioning will determine which plyometric exercises would be appropriate for you.

The exercises listed in the power section (see pages 86–91) can also be considered as plyometric exercises. One form of advanced training called "complex training" involves completing a strength exercise followed by a power exercise of a similar pattern using the same muscle groups. The strength exercise helps to increase neural drive to the muscle, which the power exercise can then utilize to generate more power than normal. An example would be completing a barbell lunge followed by a jump lunge with a twist.

The volume of plyometric exercises required depends on your sport, phase of training, and level of training experience. The table above illustrates an example of the volume of plyometric exercises you may use during the year.

PLYOMETRIC DRILLS

STANDING JUMP AND REACH

Tips for good form:
· From the half-squat position, drive your feet through the floor and your hips forward.
· Drive your arms forward and up overhead.
· Ensure triple extension of ankles, knees, and hips.

Basic description:
· Explode upward as if reaching for a target or object.

STARTING POSITION
· Stand with feet shoulder-width apart.
· Drop into a half-squat, arms extended back.

ANALYSIS OF MOVEMENT	JOINTS	JOINT MOVEMENT	MOBILIZING MUSCLES
Joint 1	Shoulder	Flexion	Deltoid (anterior fibers), pectoralis major (upper fibers), biceps brachii
Joint 2	Scapula	Upward rotation, abduction	Trapezius (upper and lower fibers), pectoralis minor, serratus anterior
Joint 3	Spine	Extension	Spinalis, longissimus, iliocostalis, multifidus, rotators, quadratus lumborum, semispinalis capitis, intertransversarii, interspinalis
Joint 4	Hip	Extension	Gluteus maximus, gluteus medius (posterior fibers), biceps femoris, semitendinosus, semimembranosus, adductor magnus (posterior fibers)
Joint 5	Knee	Extension	Rectus femoris, vastus medialis, vastus intermedius, vastus lateralis
Joint 6	Ankle	Plantarflexion	Gastrocnemius, soleus, tibialis posterior, peroneus longus and brevis

5-5-5 SQUAT JUMP

Tips for good form:
- Ensure that your knees stay in line with the second toe of each foot.
- Breathe through pursed lips as required.

Basic description:
- Complete five moderate-speed squats until your knees are level with your hips.
- Complete five squats as fast as you can.
- Complete five jump squats jumping as high as possible, with each squat having minimal foot contact time.

STARTING POSITION
- Stand with your feet hip-width apart holding a medicine ball that is approximately ten percent of your body-weight.

ANALYSIS OF MOVEMENT	JOINTS	JOINT MOVEMENT	STABILIZING MUSCLES
Joint 1	Hip	Down: flexion Up: extension	Gluteus maximus, gluteus medius (posterior fibers), biceps femoris, semitendinosus, semimembranosus, adductor magnus (posterior fibers)
Joint 2	Knee	Down: flexion Up: extension	Rectus femoris, vastus medialis, vastus intermedius, vastus lateralis
Joint 3	Ankle	Down: dorsiflexion Up: plantarflexion	Gastrocnemius, soleus, tibialis posterior, peroneus longus and brevis

TWO-FOOTED JUMPS LADDER DRILL

Basic description:
· Jump with both feet together landing in the first square on the ladder.
· On landing, quickly jump, with minimal foot contact time, to the next square on the ladder.
· Continue all the way along the ladder.

STARTING POSITION
· Stand facing a speed ladder, feet hip-width apart.

Tips for good form:
· Land and drive off the balls of the foot using an ankling motion.
· Use your arms to drive up on each take-off.
· As your skill develops, keep your eyes looking forward and your torso upright.

ANALYSIS OF MOVEMENT	JOINTS	JOINT MOVEMENT	MOBILIZING MUSCLES
Joint 1	Shoulder	Flexion, extension	Deltoid (anterior fibers), pectoralis major (upper fibers), biceps brachii
Joint 2	Scapula	Upward rotation, abduction	Trapezius (upper and lower fibers), pectoralis minor, serratus anterior
Joint 3	Hip	Flexion, extension	Psoas, iliacus, rectus femoris, tensor fascia lata, sartorius, adductor brevis, longus and magnus, gluteus medius (anterior fibers), gluteus minimus, gluteus maximus, gluteus medius (posterior fibers), biceps femoris, semitendinosus, semimembranosus, adductor magnus (posterior fibers)
Joint 4	Knee	Flexion, extension	Rectus femoris, vastus medialis, vastus intermedius, vastus lateralis
Joint 5	Ankle	Plantarflexion, dorsiflexion	Gastrocnemius, soleus, tibialis posterior, peroneus longus and brevis

SIDE-TO-SIDE BOX SHUFFLE

Basic description:
- Jump as high as possible, driving off your leg on the box, and ensuring triple extension of ankle, knee, and hip.
- Use a double-arm shift to aid elevation. Land on the mid- to fore foot of the opposite foot on the step, and the outside foot on the floor.
- On contact with the box jump back up as quickly as possible, driving off the foot on the box and aiming to jump as high as possible.

STARTING POSITION
- Begin with one foot on the box, the other foot on the floor lateral to the box, with your torso upright.

Tips for good form:
- Ensure that your knees stay in line with the second toe of the foot on landing and take-off.
- Minimize contact time with the box and floor and maximize time spent in the air.
- Breathe through pursed lips as required.

ANALYSIS OF MOVEMENT	JOINTS	JOINT MOVEMENT	MOBILIZING MUSCLES
Joint 1	Shoulder	Flexion, extension	Deltoid (anterior fibers), pectoralis major (upper fibers), biceps brachii
Joint 2	Scapula	Upward rotation, abduction	Trapezius (upper and lower fibers), pectoralis minor, serratus anterior
Joint 3	Hip	Extension, adduction	Gluteus maximus, gluteus medius (posterior fibers), biceps femoris, semitendinosus, semimembranosus, adductor magnus (posterior fibers), pectineus, adductor brevis, longus and magnus, psoas major, iliacus
Joint 4	Knee	Flexion, extension	Rectus femoris, vastus medialis, vastus intermedius, vastus lateralis
Joint 5	Ankle	Plantarflexion, dorsiflexion	Gastrocnemius, soleus, tibialis posterior, peroneus longus and brevis

ALTERNATE BOUNDING WITH SINGLE ARM ACTION

Basic description:
· Run forward, bringing the front knee up to hip level with a jump on each stride.
· Bound forward on each foot strike.

STARTING POSITION
· Begin in the "ready" position.

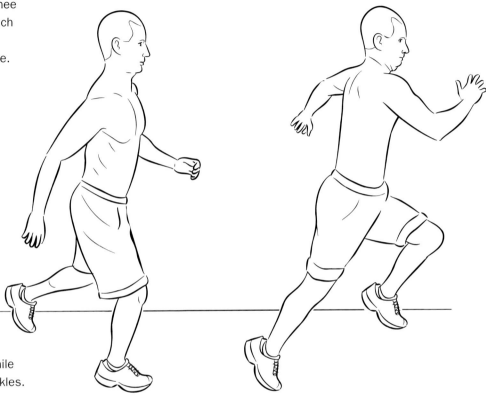

Tips for good form:
· Bounce up off each stride, ensuring triple extension.
· Use the arms in a single arm shift.
· Do not reach forward at ground contact.
· Minimize ground contact time while maintaining a stiffness in the ankles.

ANALYSIS OF MOVEMENT	JOINTS	JOINT MOVEMENT	MOBILIZING MUSCLES
Joint 1	Shoulder	Flexion, extension,	Deltoid (anterior and posterior fibers), latissimus dorsi, teres major, infraspinatus, teres minor, pectoralis major, triceps brachii (long head), biceps brachii
Joint 2	Scapula	Upward rotation, downward rotation, abduction, adduction	Trapezius, pectoralis minor, serratus anterior, levator scapula, rhomboid major and minor
Joint 3	Spine	Rotation	Ipsilateral: Internal oblique Contralateral: Multifidus, rotatores, external oblique
Joint 4	Hip	Extension, flexion	Gluteus maximus, gluteus medius, biceps femoris, semitendinosus, semimembranosus, psoas, iliacus, rectus femoris, tensor fascia lata, sartorius, adductor brevis, longus and magnus, gluteus minimus
Joint 5	Knee	Extension, flexion	Rectus femoris, vastus medialis, vastus intermedius, vastus lateralis, biceps femoris, semitendinosus, semimembranosus, gracilis, sartorius, gastrocnemius, popliteus, plantaris
Joint 6	Ankle	Plantarflexion, dorsiflexion	Gastrocnemius, soleus, tibialis posterior, peroneus longus and brevis

SINGLE LEG BOUNDING

Basic description:
- Begin hopping on one leg.
- Drive your knee up to hip level, ensuring triple extension of the ankles, knees, and hips.
- You can use a double or single arm shift.

STARTING POSITION
- Begin with a slow run.

Tips for good form:
- Minimize ground contact time and use your arms to generate lift.

ANALYSIS OF MOVEMENT	JOINTS	JOINT MOVEMENT	MOBILIZING MUSCLES
Joint 1	Shoulder	Flexion, extension,	Deltoid (anterior and posterior fibers), latissimus dorsi, teres major, infraspinatus, teres minor, pectoralis major, triceps brachii (long head), biceps brachii
Joint 2	Scapula	Upward rotation, downward rotation, abduction, adduction	Trapezius, pectoralis minor, serratus anterior, levator scapula, rhomboid major and minor
Joint 3	Spine	Rotation	Ipsilateral: internal oblique Contralateral: multifidus, rotatores, external oblique
Joint 4	Hip	Extension, flexion	Gluteus maximus, gluteus medius, biceps femoris, semitendinosus, semimembranosus, psoas, iliacus, rectus femoris, tensor fascia lata, sartorius, adductor brevis, longus and magnus, gluteus minimus
Joint 5	Knee	Extension, flexion	Rectus femoris, vastus medialis, vastus intermedius, vastus lateralis, biceps femoris, semitendinosus, semimembranosus, gracilis, sartorius, gastrocnemius, popliteus, plantaris
Joint 6	Ankle	Plantarflexion, dorsiflexion	Gastrocnemius, soleus, tibialis posterior, peroneus longus and brevis

FRONT BOX JUMP

Basic description:
· Drop into a quarter-squat and jump on to the box.
· Land with both feet simultaneously as softly as possible.
· Step down and repeat 8–10 times.

STARTING POSITION
· Stand facing a box 12–42 in (30–107 cm) high with feet shoulder-width apart

Tips for good form:
· Use your arms to help the "lift" from the floor.
· Land with knees directly in line with the second toes.
· Bend at the hip, knee, and ankle to soften the impact.

ANALYSIS OF MOVEMENT	JOINTS	JOINT MOVEMENT	MOBILIZING MUSCLES
Joint 1	Shoulder	Flexion, extension,	Deltoid (anterior fibers), pectoralis major (upper fibers), biceps brachii
Joint 2	Scapula	Upward rotation, abduction, elevation	Trapezius (upper and lower fibers), pectoralis minor, serratus anterior, levator scapula
Joint 3	Hip	Flexion, extension	Gluteus maximus, gluteus medius (posterior fibers), biceps femoris, semitendinosus, semimembranosus, adductor magnus (posterior fibers)
Joint 4	Knee	Flexion, extension	Rectus femoris, vastus medialis, vastus intermedius, vastus lateralis
Joint 5	Ankle	Plantarflexion, dorsiflexion	Gastrocnemius, soleus, tibialis posterior, peroneus longus and brevis

JUMP FROM BOX

Tips for good form:
· On landing, ensure the knees stay in line with the second toes.

Basic description:
· Step (don't jump) from the box.
· Land with feet shoulder-width apart, quickly absorbing the landing.

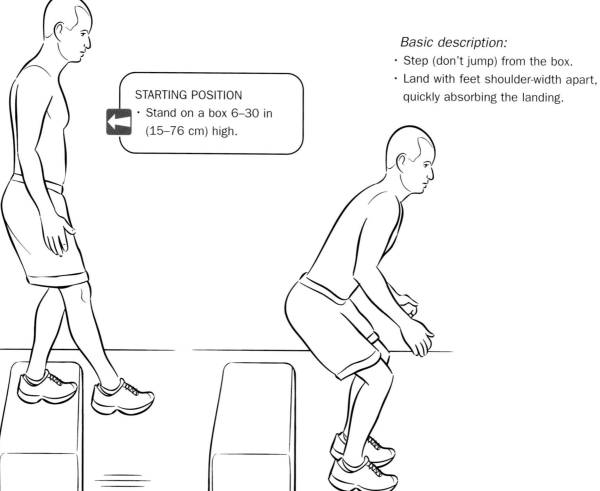

STARTING POSITION
· Stand on a box 6–30 in (15–76 cm) high.

ANALYSIS OF MOVEMENT	JOINTS	JOINT MOVEMENT	MOBILIZING MUSCLES
Joint 1	Shoulder	Flexion	Deltoid (anterior fibers), pectoralis major (upper fibers), biceps brachii
Joint 2	Scapula	Upward rotation, abduction, elevation	Trapezius (upper and lower fibers), pectoralis minor, serratus anterior, levator scapula
Joint 3	Hip	Flexion	Eccentric contraction: gluteus maximus, gluteus medius (posterior fibers), biceps femoris, semitendinosus, semimembranosus, adductor magnus (posterior fibers)
Joint 4	Knee	Flexion	Eccentric contraction: rectus femoris, vastus medialis, vastus intermedius, vastus lateralis
Joint 5	Ankle	Dorsiflexion	Eccentric contraction: gastrocnemius, soleus, tibialis posterior, peroneus longus and brevis

DEPTH JUMP

Basic description:

· Step (don't jump) off the box, landing on both feet.
· Anticipate the landing, and jump up as quickly and as high as possible.

Tips for good form:

· Ensure the knees remain in line with the second toes on landing and take-off.
· Minimize the ground contact time.
· Ensure triple extension of the ankles, knees, and hips.

STARTING POSITION
· Stand on a box 6–24 in (15–60 cm) high.

ANALYSIS OF MOVEMENT	JOINTS	JOINT MOVEMENT	MOBILIZING MUSCLES
Joint 1	Shoulder	Flexion, extension	Deltoid (anterior fibers), pectoralis major (upper fibers), biceps brachii
Joint 2	Scapula	Upward rotation, abduction, elevation, downward rotation, adduction, depression	Trapezius (upper and lower fibers), pectoralis minor, serratus anterior, levator scapula
Joint 3	Hip	Flexion, extension	Gluteus maximus, gluteus medius (posterior fibers), biceps femoris, semitendinosus, semimembranosus, adductor magnus (posterior fibers)
Joint 4	Knee	Flexion, extension	Rectus femoris, vastus medialis, vastus intermedius, vastus lateralis
Joint 5	Ankle	Plantarflexion, dorsiflexion	Gastrocnemius, soleus, tibialis posterior, peroneus longus and brevis

SPEED

Many sports require the ability to run at top speed, with game situations often won or lost by the ability to shift into top gear. If your sport requires top-end speed or fast acceleration, a speed-training program can play a major role in helping you to achieve optimal performance.

To achieve your speed potential, there are a number of factors that require attention. These factors are strength (see pages 80–85), power (see pages 86–91), flexibility (see pages 25–38), acceleration, stride length, stride frequency, and running technique.

To accelerate, you need to increase in stride length and stride frequency. To increase stride length and frequency, an increase in whole body strength is required. This increase in strength allows for a greater force generation and a shorter ground contact time.

It should be noted that the greatest increase in speed (acceleration) is achieved in the first eight to ten strides, while maximum speed generally takes four to five seconds to achieve. This is important when designing your conditioning program. To minimize the time taken to reach top speed, rapid strides should gradually increase in length until your full stride length is achieved.

Stride length and frequency are interrelated in such a way that an over-increase of one will lead to a decrease in the other, causing a reduction of speed. Optimal stride length has been shown to be 2.3 to 2.5 times longer than the athlete's leg at maximal speed, and it is achieved as running technique, strength, and power increases. Optimal stride length can be improved by improving sprint technique, absolute strength (see pages 80–85), power (see pages 86–91), and plyometric ability (see pages 102–111).

A good sprinting technique (also called sprinting mechanics) increases neuromuscular efficiency, which allows for smooth, co-ordinated movements that contribute to faster running speeds. Jamaican sprinters Usain Bolt and Asafa Powell are the two fastest men of all time, and they both have a very smooth, co-ordinated sprinting technique.

There are three main elements to a good sprinting technique: posture, arm action, and leg action. Posture refers predominantly to the position of the torso. In acceleration, the torso leans forward at approximately 45° to help overcome inertia. As you increase toward your top speed the torso moves upright, reaching about 80° when you are running flat out.

Arm action works as a counter-rotation to the large forces generated by the legs, and the arm action should be greatest during acceleration. The leg during the propulsive phase of gait is required to achieve full extension of the ankle, knee, and hip joints. The height of knee lift during the swing phase is lower during acceleration and higher at top speeds.

Speed training

The speed drills in this section allow the development of stride frequency and acceleration. Top speed development can be achieved by sprinting for at least five seconds in the drills that include sprints (see pages 121–123).

Speed sessions should always be carried out after adequate rest and without any muscular soreness. Optimal speed can only be achieved while sprinting in a relaxed manner, and recovery times between drills should be long enough for the heart rate to return to normal resting levels. Speed endurance can be achieved using longer runs or using shorter rest periods. A full warm-up (see pages 39–47) should be carried out prior to speed training, including the sprint drills to be performed at a sub-maximal level.

SPEED DRILLS

ANKLING

Basic description:
- With "stiff" ankles, begin jogging on the spot or slowly forward.
- Use small steps, landing and pushing off on the balls of the feet.

Tips for good form:
- Use minimal ground contact time.
- Drive the arms as you would if running.

STARTING POSITION
- Stand with feet hip-width apart.

ANALYSIS OF MOVEMENT	JOINTS	JOINT MOVEMENT	MOBILIZING MUSCLES
Joint 1	Shoulder	Flexion, extension	Deltoid (anterior fibers), pectoralis major (upper fibers), biceps brachii
Joint 2	Scapula	Upward rotation, abduction, downward rotation, adduction	Trapezius (upper and lower fibers), pectoralis minor, serratus anterior
Joint 3	Ankle	Plantarflexion, dorsiflexion	Gastrocnemius, soleus, tibialis posterior, peroneus longus and brevis

BUTT KICKERS

Basic description:
- Begin jogging slowly. As you increase your speed, ensure that you pull your heels up to your backside and your knee up to hip level. Keep your torso upright and drive your arms.

Tips for good form:
- Keep your torso upright and ensure that you don't stride too far forward.
- Drive the arms as you would if running.

STARTING POSITION
- Slow jogging.

ANALYSIS OF MOVEMENT	JOINTS	JOINT MOVEMENT	MOBILIZING MUSCLES
Joint 1	Shoulder	Flexion, extension	Deltoid (anterior and posterior fibers), pectoralis major (upper fibers), biceps brachii, deltoid (posterior fibers), latissimus dorsi, teres major, infraspinatus, teres minor, pectoralis major (lower fibers), triceps brachii (long head)
Joint 2	Scapulothoracic	Upward rotation, abduction, downward rotation, adduction	Trapezius, rhomboids, pectoralis minor, serratus anterior, levator scapula
Joint 3	Hip	Flexion, extension	Psoas, iliacus, tensor fascia lata, sartorius, adductors group, gluteus maximus, gluteus medius, gluteus minimus, biceps femoris, semitendinosus, semimembranosus
Joint 4	Knee	Flexion, extension	Quadriceps group, hamstrings group, sartorius, gracilis, gastrocnemius
Joint 5	Ankle	Plantarflexion, dorsiflexion	Gastrocnemius, soleus, plantaris, tibialis posterior, peroneus longus and brevis, tibialis anterior, flexor digitorum longus, flexor hallucis longus, extensor digitorum longus, extensor hallucis longus

LADDER SPEED RUN

Tips for good form:
· Emphasize a high knee position and make sure that ground contact is minimal.
· As your technique improves, increase your foot speed. Keep your torso and head upright.
· Drive the arms as you would if running.

Basic description:
· Run through the speed ladder, touching down both feet quickly in each square.

STARTING POSITION
· Stand in the "ready" position in front of a speed ladder.

ANALYSIS OF MOVEMENT	JOINTS	JOINT MOVEMENT	MOBILIZING MUSCLES
Joint 1	Shoulder	Flexion, extension	Deltoid (anterior and posterior fibers), latissimus dorsi, teres major, infraspinatus, teres minor, pectoralis major, triceps brachii (long head), biceps brachii
Joint 2	Scapula	Upward rotation, downward rotation, abduction, adduction	Trapezius, pectoralis minor, serratus anterior, levator scapula, rhomboid major and minor
Joint 3	Spine	Rotation	Ipsilateral: internal oblique Contralateral: multifidus, rotatores, external oblique
Joint 4	Hip	Extension, flexion	Gluteus maximus, gluteus medius, biceps femoris, semitendinosus, semimembranosus, psoas, iliacus, rectus femoris, tensor fascia lata, sartorius, adductor brevis, longus and magnus, gluteus minimus
Joint 5	Knee	Extension, flexion	Rectus femoris, vastus medialis, vastus intermedius, vastus lateralis, biceps femoris, semitendinosus, semimembranosus, gracilis, sartorius, gastrocnemius, popliteus, plantaris
Joint 6	Ankle	Plantarflexion, dorsiflexion	Gastrocnemius, soleus, tibialis posterior, peroneus longus and brevis, Gastrocnemius, soleus, tibialis posterior, peroneus longus and brevis

LADDER STRIDE RUN

Basic description:
· Run through the speed ladder as
  fast as possible, touching down
  one foot in each square.

Tips for good form:
· Emphasize a high knee position, arm
  drive, triple extension, and ensure that
  ground contact is minimal.
· As your technique improves, increase your
  foot speed. Keep your torso and head
  upright at all times.
· Drive the arms as you would if running.

> STARTING POSITION
> · Stand in the "ready"
>   position in front of a
>   speed ladder.

ANALYSIS OF MOVEMENT	JOINTS	JOINT MOVEMENT	MOBILIZING MUSCLES
Joint 1	Shoulder	Flexion, extension,	Deltoid (anterior and posterior fibers), latissimus dorsi, teres major, infraspinatus, teres minor, pectoralis major, triceps brachii (long head), biceps brachii
Joint 2	Scapula	Upward rotation, downward rotation, abduction, adduction	Trapezius, pectoralis minor, serratus anterior, levator scapula, rhomboid major and minor
Joint 3	Spine	Rotation	Ipsilateral: internal oblique Contralateral: multifidus, rotatores, external oblique
Joint 4	Hip	Extension, flexion	Gluteus maximus, gluteus medius, biceps femoris, semitendinosus, semimembranosus, psoas, iliacus, rectus femoris, tensor fascia lata, sartorius, adductor brevis, longus and magnus, gluteus minimus
Joint 5	Knee	Extension, flexion	Rectus femoris, vastus medialis, vastus intermedius, vastus lateralis, biceps femoris, semitendinosus, semimembranosus, gracilis, sartorius, gastrocnemius, popliteus, plantaris
Joint 6	Ankle	Plantarflexion, dorsiflexion	Gastrocnemius, soleus, tibialis posterior, peroneus longus and brevis

HURDLE FAST LEGS

Basic description:
- Start by hurdling with the left leg over the first hurdle on the left, then take two quick steps before hurdling the first hurdle on the right with the right leg.
- Continue the same sequence along all the hurdles.

Tips for good form:
- Emphasize a high knee position, arm drive, triple extension, and ensure that ground contact is minimal.
- As your technique improves, increase your foot speed. Keep your torso and head upright at all times.
- Drive the arms as you would if running.

STARTING POSITION
- Stand in the "ready" position in front of four or five 6–12 in (15–30 cm) hurdles staggered in two lines, one in front of the left leg, the other in front of the right leg.

ANALYSIS OF MOVEMENT	JOINTS	JOINT MOVEMENT	MOBILIZING MUSCLES
Joint 1	Shoulder	Flexion, extension	Deltoid (anterior and posterior fibers), latissimus dorsi, teres major, infraspinatus, teres minor, pectoralis major, triceps brachii (long head), biceps brachii
Joint 2	Scapula	Upward rotation, downward rotation, abduction, adduction	Trapezius, pectoralis minor, serratus anterior, levator scapula, rhomboid major and minor
Joint 3	Spine	Rotation	Ipsilateral: internal oblique Contralateral: multifidus, rotatores, external oblique
Joint 4	Hip	Extension, flexion	Gluteus maximus, gluteus medius, biceps femoris, semitendinosus, semimembranosus, psoas, iliacus, rectus femoris, tensor fascia lata, sartorius, adductor brevis, longus and magnus, gluteus minimus
Joint 5	Knee	Extension, flexion	Rectus femoris, vastus medialis, vastus intermedius, vastus lateralis, biceps femoris, semitendinosus, semimembranosus, gracilis, sartorius, gastrocnemius, popliteus, plantaris
Joint 6	Ankle	Plantarflexion, dorsiflexion	Gastrocnemius, soleus, tibialis posterior, peroneus longus and brevis

SINGLE LEG HURDLE RUN-THROUGH

Basic description:
· Run with one leg outside the hurdles and the other leg going over the hurdles.
· The outside leg stays straight as it passes the hurdles in a shuffling manner.

STARTING POSITION
· Stand in the "ready" position in front of eight or ten 6–12 in (15–30 cm) hurdles about 3 ft (1 m) apart.

Tips for good form:
· Use an explosive high knee lift on the hurdling leg.
· Keep the torso and head upright.
· Use a short ground contact time on the hurdling leg.
· Drive the arms as you would if running.

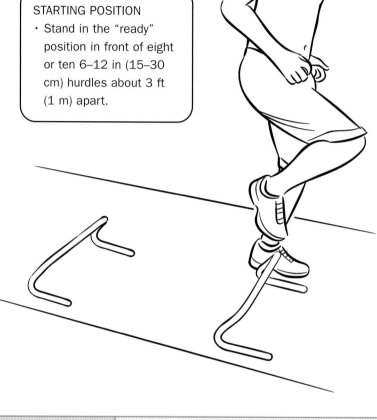

ANALYSIS OF MOVEMENT	JOINTS	JOINT MOVEMENT	MOBILIZING MUSCLES
Joint 1	Shoulder	Flexion, extension	Deltoid (anterior and posterior fibers), latissimus dorsi, teres major, infraspinatus, teres minor, pectoralis major, triceps brachii (long head), biceps brachii
Joint 2	Scapula	Upward rotation, downward rotation, abduction, adduction	Trapezius, pectoralis minor, serratus anterior, levator scapula, rhomboid major and minor
Joint 3	Spine	Rotation	Ipsilateral: internal oblique Contralateral: multifidus, rotatores, external oblique
Joint 4	Hip	Extension, flexion	Gluteus maximus, gluteus medius, biceps femoris, semitendinosus, semimembranosus, psoas, iliacus, rectus femoris, tensor fascia lata, sartorius, adductor brevis, longus and magnus, gluteus minimus
Joint 5	Knee	Extension, flexion	Rectus femoris, vastus medialis, vastus intermedius, vastus lateralis, biceps femoris, semitendinosus, semimembranosus, gracilis, sartorius, gastrocnemius, popliteus, plantaris
Joint 6	Ankle	Plantarflexion, dorsiflexion	Gastrocnemius, soleus, tibialis posterior, peroneus longus and brevis

HURDLE RUN-THROUGH

Tips for good form:

· Use an explosive high knee lift on the hurdling leg, with a heel-to-gluteus recovery.
· Keep the torso and head upright.
· Use a short ground contact time on the hurdling leg.
· Drive the arms as you would if running.

Basic description:

· Run over the hurdles with a one or two foot strike between each hurdle.

> STARTING POSITION
> · Stand in the "ready" position in front of eight or ten 6–12 in (15–30 cm) hurdles about 3 ft (1 m) apart.

ANALYSIS OF MOVEMENT	JOINTS	JOINT MOVEMENT	MOBILIZING MUSCLES
Joint 1	Shoulder	Flexion, extension	Deltoid (anterior and posterior fibers), latissimus dorsi, teres major, infraspinatus, teres minor, pectoralis major, triceps brachii (long head), biceps brachii
Joint 2	Scapula	Upward rotation, downward rotation, abduction, adduction	Trapezius, pectoralis minor, serratus anterior, levator scapula, rhomboid major and minor
Joint 3	Spine	Rotation	Ipsilateral: internal oblique Contralateral: multifidus, rotatores, external oblique
Joint 4	Hip	Extension, flexion	Gluteus maximus, gluteus medius, biceps femoris, semitendinosus, semimembranosus, psoas, iliacus, rectus femoris, tensor fascia lata, sartorius, adductor brevis, longus and magnus, gluteus minimus
Joint 5	Knee	Extension, flexion	Rectus femoris, vastus medialis, vastus intermedius, vastus lateralis, biceps femoris, semitendinosus, semimembranosus, gracilis, sartorius, gastrocnemius, popliteus, plantaris
Joint 6	Ankle	Plantarflexion, dorsiflexion	Gastrocnemius, soleus, tibialis posterior, peroneus longus and brevis

FALLING STARTS

Tips for good form:
- Delay the first leg drive as long as possible.
- Explosively use the arms to aid forward drive.
- Use quick feet and small strides.

Basic description:
- Go up onto tip-toes and begin falling forward as far as you can.
- Before losing your balance, drive one knee up explosively and begin accelerating into a sprint over a few yards before stopping.
- Complete 10–12 repetitions, alternating the lead leg each time.

STARTING POSITION
- Stand with feet hip-width apart.

ANALYSIS OF MOVEMENT	JOINTS	JOINT MOVEMENT	MOBILIZING MUSCLES
Joint 1	Shoulder	Flexion, extension	Deltoid (anterior and posterior fibers), latissimus dorsi, teres major, infraspinatus, teres minor, pectoralis major, triceps brachii (long head), biceps brachii
Joint 2	Scapula	Upward rotation, downward rotation, abduction, adduction	Trapezius, pectoralis minor, serratus anterior, levator scapula, rhomboid major and minor
Joint 3	Spine	Rotation	Ipsilateral: internal oblique Contralateral: multifidus, rotatores, external oblique
Joint 4	Hip	Extension, flexion	Gluteus maximus, gluteus medius, biceps femoris, semitendinosus, semimembranosus, psoas, iliacus, rectus femoris, tensor fascia lata, sartorius, adductor brevis, longus and magnus, gluteus minimus
Joint 5	Knee	Extension, flexion	Rectus femoris, vastus medialis, vastus intermedius, vastus lateralis, biceps femoris, semitendinosus, semimembranosus, gracilis, sartorius, gastrocnemius, popliteus, plantaris
Joint 6	Ankle	Plantarflexion, dorsiflexion	Gastrocnemius, soleus, tibialis posterior, peroneus longus and brevis

ANKLING TO SPRINT

Basic description:
· Begin ankling for 16–33 ft (5–10 m)—see
  page 113.
· At the end of the ankling, gradually increase
  your speed until top speed is reached.
· Maintain top speed for 1–5 seconds.

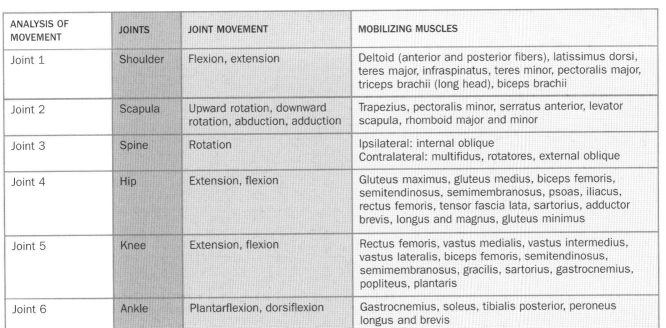

STARTING POSITION
· Stand with feet hip-
  width apart.

Tips for good form:
· Emphasize stiff ankles
  and torso.
· Use triple extension
  of ankles, knees, and
  hips, and arm drive on
  the sprint.
· Minimize ground
  contact time.
· Use a high knee lift
  as you approach
  top speed.

ANALYSIS OF MOVEMENT	JOINTS	JOINT MOVEMENT	MOBILIZING MUSCLES
Joint 1	Shoulder	Flexion, extension	Deltoid (anterior and posterior fibers), latissimus dorsi, teres major, infraspinatus, teres minor, pectoralis major, triceps brachii (long head), biceps brachii
Joint 2	Scapula	Upward rotation, downward rotation, abduction, adduction	Trapezius, pectoralis minor, serratus anterior, levator scapula, rhomboid major and minor
Joint 3	Spine	Rotation	Ipsilateral: internal oblique Contralateral: multifidus, rotatores, external oblique
Joint 4	Hip	Extension, flexion	Gluteus maximus, gluteus medius, biceps femoris, semitendinosus, semimembranosus, psoas, iliacus, rectus femoris, tensor fascia lata, sartorius, adductor brevis, longus and magnus, gluteus minimus
Joint 5	Knee	Extension, flexion	Rectus femoris, vastus medialis, vastus intermedius, vastus lateralis, biceps femoris, semitendinosus, semimembranosus, gracilis, sartorius, gastrocnemius, popliteus, plantaris
Joint 6	Ankle	Plantarflexion, dorsiflexion	Gastrocnemius, soleus, tibialis posterior, peroneus longus and brevis

HURDLE RUN-THROUGH TO SPRINT

Basic description:
- Begin by completing a hurdle run-through (see page 119).
- At the end of the this, accelerate into a sprint until top speed is reached.
- Maintain your top speed for 1–5 seconds.

Tips for good form:
- Emphasize stiff ankles and torso.
- Use triple extension of ankles, knees, and hips and arm drive on the sprint.
- Minimize ground contact time.
- Use a high knee lift through the hurdles and as you approach top speed.

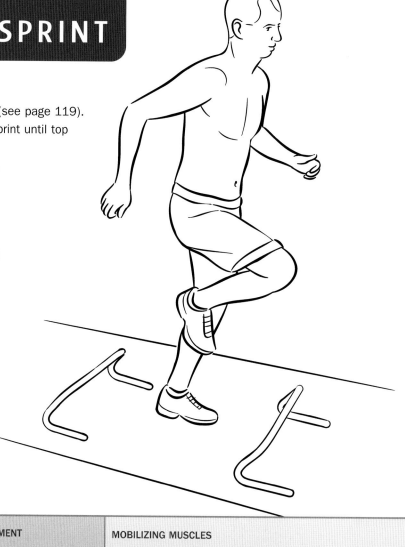

STARTING POSITION
- Stand in the "ready" position in front of eight or ten 6–12 in (15–30 cm) hurdles about 3 ft (1 m) apart.

ANALYSIS OF MOVEMENT	JOINTS	JOINT MOVEMENT	MOBILIZING MUSCLES
Joint 1	Shoulder	Flexion, extension	Deltoid (anterior and posterior fibers), latissimus dorsi, teres major, infraspinatus, teres minor, pectoralis major, triceps brachii (long head), biceps brachii
Joint 2	Scapula	Upward rotation, downward rotation, abduction, adduction	Trapezius, pectoralis minor, serratus anterior, levator scapula, rhomboid major and minor
Joint 3	Spine	Rotation	Ipsilateral: internal oblique Contralateral: multifidus, rotatores, external oblique
Joint 4	Hip	Extension, flexion	Gluteus maximus, gluteus medius, biceps femoris, semitendinosus, semimembranosus, psoas, iliacus, rectus femoris, tensor fascia lata, sartorius, adductor brevis, longus and magnus, gluteus minimus
Joint 5	Knee	Extension, flexion	Rectus femoris, vastus medialis, vastus intermedius, vastus lateralis, biceps femoris, semitendinosus, semimembranosus, gracilis, sartorius, gastrocnemius, popliteus, plantaris
Joint 6	Ankle	Plantarflexion, dorsiflexion	Gastrocnemius, soleus, tibialis posterior, peroneus longus and brevis

ANKLING TO HURDLE RUN-THROUGH TO SPRINT

Basic description:
· Begin ankling (see page 113) for 16 ft (5 m), then immediately complete a hurdle run-through (see page 119).
· At the end of the hurdle run-through, accelerate into a sprint until top speed is reached.
· Maintain top speed for 1–5 seconds.

Tips for good form:
· Emphasize stiff ankles and torso.
· Use triple extension of ankles, knees, and hips, and arm drive on the sprint.
· Minimize ground contact time.
· Use a high knee lift through the hurdles and as you approach your top speed.

STARTING POSITION
· Stand in the "ready" position 16–20 ft (5–6 m) in front of eight or ten 6–12 in (15–30 cm) hurdles about 3 ft (1 m) apart.

ANALYSIS OF MOVEMENT	JOINTS	JOINT MOVEMENT	MOBILIZING MUSCLES
Joint 1	Shoulder	Flexion, extension	Deltoid (anterior and posterior fibers), latissimus dorsi, teres major, infraspinatus, teres minor, pectoralis major, triceps brachii (long head), biceps brachii
Joint 2	Scapula	Upward rotation, downward rotation, abduction, adduction	Trapezius, pectoralis minor, serratus anterior, levator scapula, rhomboid major and minor
Joint 3	Spine	Rotation	Ipsilateral: internal oblique Contralateral: multifidus, rotatores, external oblique
Joint 4	Hip	Extension, flexion	Gluteus maximus, gluteus medius, biceps femoris, semitendinosus, semimembranosus, psoas, iliacus, rectus femoris, tensor fascia lata, sartorius, adductor brevis, longus and magnus, gluteus minimus
Joint 5	Knee	Extension, flexion	Rectus femoris, vastus medialis, vastus intermedius, vastus lateralis, biceps femoris, semitendinosus, semimembranosus, gracilis, sartorius, gastrocnemius, popliteus, plantaris
Joint 6	Ankle	Plantarflexion, dorsiflexion	Gastrocnemius, soleus, tibialis posterior, peroneus longus and brevis

DESIGNING YOUR PROGRAM

Before designing your speed development program, there are a number of factors that you need to take into consideration. To begin with, you must perform a needs analysis, which will give you all the information you require to design your program.

Your needs analysis will include:

1. Your age
2. Training age
3. Training experience
4. Surface on which you'll play the sport
5. Environment
6. Contact
7. Strength qualities
8. Biomotor abilities
9. Energy system requirement
10. SMART goal setting

Each of these factors will determine what training you do, where you start, how you do it, how often, how much rest you need in between sessions, and where to focus your training.

Almost all sports require training through the following continuum:

1. Flexibility/stability
2. Strength
3. Power
4. Speed

This means that you must build a strong foundation of good flexibility and stability of joints. This will help to minimize the likelihood of injury when the training gets serious, and enables maximum power output of the muscles, and full transference of forces across the joints to create quick movement.

Beginner athletes (training age less than one year) should begin with the beginner Primal Pattern® Movement exercises for a minimum of 4–6 weeks. These exercises should only be progressed to the intermediate level once the maximum number of sets and reps can be completed with perfect form.

Intermediate athletes (training age one to two years) can start with the beginner or intermediate Primal Pattern® Movement exercises for at least three to four weeks. These exercises should only be progressed to the advanced level once the maximum number of sets and reps can be completed with perfect form.

Advanced level athletes (training age over two years) can start with the beginner, intermediate, or advanced Primal Pattern® Movement exercises for at least two to three weeks. The program should only be progressed to maximal strength training once the maximum number of sets and reps of the advanced Primal Pattern® exercises can be completed with perfect form.

Maximal strength training can begin once you have at least one to two years of consistent weight-training experience, and can complete the intermediate Primal Pattern® Movement exercises with perfect form. It has been suggested that power training is safe to commence once you are able to back squat one and a half times your body weight. It may be possible to begin some power exercises sooner under professional supervision, but this is a safe rule to follow if not.

Exercise Variables

Exercise variables are the loading parameters used during each lift or exercise in a training session. Exercise variables include the speed of movement (tempo), repetitions completed, rest period between sets, and the intensity, which is often measured in terms of percentage of a one repetition maximum (1 RM).

The two tables below illustrate how exercise variables can be manipulated to achieve a desired physiological effect.

Loading parameters * OTUT = optimal time under tension

FIBER TYPE	% 1 RM	OTUT*	RECOVERY	TIME TO FATIGUE	RESPONSE
Type I	0–40%	> 70 secs	1–2mins	3–5 mins	Aerobic
Type IIA	40–70%	40–70 secs	2–3mins	30–120 secs	Hypertrophy
Type IIB	70–100%	< 20 secs	3–5mins	12–15 secs	Neural

Loading parameters (adapted from *CHEK Exercise Coach Certification Manual*)

PHYSIOLOGICAL EFFECT	TIME UNDER TENSION/INTENSITY	MUSCLE FIBER TYPE
Tonic effect	3–3.5 minutes	Type I
Strength endurance	100–180 secs	Type I & type IIA
Strength	40–70 secs	Type IIA
Maximal strength (mass)	> 90% 1 RM	Type IIA & IIB
Power (acceleration)	< 20 secs	Type IIB

So how do you select the correct parameters for each exercise? The table (right) provides a guide to how you may wish to select the loading parameters for each workout.

* Intensity refers to percentage of 1 RM of that exercise, weight of medicine ball (as percentage of body weight), or level of exercise load (low–high).

** Tempo refers to the number of seconds taken to move the resistance. "10s/10s" means contract for 10 seconds then relax for 10 seconds or contract for 10 seconds, then contract the other side for 10 seconds where applicable. "2–0–2" means lift the weight in two seconds and lower the weight in two seconds. "Explosive" means move the resistance or body part as quickly as possible.

Suggested loading parameters for your workouts

EXERCISE	REST PERIOD	INTENSITY*	REPS	SETS	TEMPO**
Four-point tummy vacuum	1 minute	Body weight	10	1–3	10s/10s
Horse stance	1 minute	Body weight	10	1–3	10s/10s
Primal Pattern® Movements (beginner)	1–2 minutes	75% 1 RM	12–15	2–4	3–0–3
Primal Pattern® Movements (intermediate)	1–2 minutes	80% 1 RM	10–12	2–4	2–0–2
Primal Pattern® Movements (advanced)	1–2 minutes	80% 1 RM	10–12	2–4	1–0–2
Maximal strength	3–5 minutes	90–95% 1 RM	3–5	3–5	1–0–2
Power	3–5 minutes	5–10% bodyweight or 50–75% 1 RM	8–10	3–5	Explosive
Agility drills	1:3–1:4 work/rest ratio	Maximum	<10 secs	3–5	Explosive
Plyometric drills	3–5 minutes	Low–high	<10 secs	3–5	Explosive
Speed drills	3–5 minutes	Maximum	<10 secs	3–5	Explosive

NEEDS ANALYSIS: GOAL-SETTING

Like going on any journey, before you begin training you need to map out your route. And before you can do this, you need to know where you are starting and where you aim to finish. In this analogy, the finish is your ultimate goal. Whether your goal is to win an Olympic gold medal or complete a marathon, you need to know exactly what you are hoping to achieve.

Not only can you set competition goals once you know this, but you can also set training goals. For instance, a basketball player may set time goals for completing specific agility or speed drills in accordance with the movement patterns in basketball.

Whenever you set goals, they need to be SMART. SMART stands for:

· **S**pecific
· **M**easurable
· **A**chievable, yet challenging
· **R**egularly reviewed
· **T**imed

Specific requires the goal to be described in the smallest common denominator. For example, "to win the 100-meter regional championships in June this year in a time of 11.90 seconds or quicker."

Measurable requires a number that can be measured. In the above example a time of 11.90 seconds can be measured. This means that training time goals can also be set and progress can be monitored.

Achievable, yet challenging means that the goals should be approximately 50 percent achievable. If a goal is too difficult or too easy, motivation is difficult to maintain.

Regularly reviewed means that you should have incremental goals set in place along the way toward your ultimate goal. On a regular basis (weekly or monthly), your shorter term goals can be reviewed and assessed, and your progress can be evaluated.

A **Timed** goal requires a specific time by which to achieve the goal. Without a time goal, motivation and focus is difficult to maintain and the training plan would be difficult, if not impossible, to design effectively.

Outcome goals are the goals that you wish to achieve, for example, "win the 100-meter title.'

Process goals are the things you aim to do along the way to achieve the outcome goal. For example, "train six times per week for 45 to 60 minutes, stretch every evening for 10 minutes, eat as advised each meal time, go to bed by 10 p.m. every evening, and get at least eight hours sleep per night."

NEEDS ANALYSIS

Your age

Your age needs to be taken into consideration because as we age we tend to require more recovery in between training sessions.

Training age

Your training age is the number of years that you have consistently taken part in a resistance exercise program as part of your training regime. For instance, if you have been weight-training with no interruptions for five years, then your training age would be five. The higher your training age, the closer to your genetic potential you are likely to be. Therefore, the more advanced your program needs to be, the shorter you stay in each phase, and the smaller your increments of progress are likely to be, for example the increases in weight lifted.

Training experience

Your training experience determines what type of program you will be able to handle, and how quickly you might progress. For instance, at school I competed in soccer, basketball, badminton, cross-country running, cricket, 100, 200, and 400 meters, long jump, triple jump, and volleyball. Non-competitively I also swam, rode a bike, and played tennis, softball, table tennis, squash, snooker, and pool. As you can see, I played a wide variety of sports, and therefore developed a well-rounded skill set.

On the other hand, if you have only played basketball, while you may be great at that one sport, you may not have such a well-rounded skill set and may not develop as quickly as others.

Surface of the sport

The surface on which the sport is practiced or played may determine how much balance and functional strength you will require in your training. For instance a downhill skier, a gymnast, or surfer will require a lot more balance than a sprinter, soccer player, basketball player, or volleyball player.

The more balance required for your particular sport, the more you may wish to add single leg exercises or even introduce uneven surfaces to train on, such as wobble boards and swiss balls.

STRENGTH QUALITIES

There are different qualities of strenth. These are:

- Isometric
- Concentric
- Eccentric
- Isokinetic

Isometric means "without movement." This is where there is muscular contraction without any movement across the joint. This often occurs when opposing muscles contract to stabilize a joint, or when the muscle is contracting against an external object, such as a person or a wall. Gymnasts often use isometric movements to hold static positions in between fast movements.

Concentric muscular contractions occur when the muscle or muscles overcome a load (weight, object, and/or gravity), and the muscle is shortening. Concentric contractions are often responsible for acceleration. Concentric contractions in weight training normally occur in the lifting of the weight.

Eccentric muscular contractions occur when the muscle or muscles slow down the momentum of a load (weight, object, and/or force of gravity), and the muscle is lengthening. Eccentric contractions are often responsible for deceleration. Eccentric contractions in weight training normally occur in the lowering of the weight.

Isokinetic means "same speed." There is no instance in nature in which our bodies move at constant speeds. The closest we ever get to it is in activities such as swimming, rowing, canoeing, and kayaking as we pull the water with our hands or oars at a reasonably consistent speed.

Once you understand the different strength qualities of your sport, you can decide which qualities you need and in what proportions. For instance, you may decide that as a rugby player you require predominantly concentric and eccentric strength for movement, kicking, tackling, scrummaging, and passing, with a small proportion of isometric strength for the scrum.

BIOMOTOR ABILITIES

To enable you to focus the right amount of time in the right areas of your program, analyzing your biomotor ability profile can be a very beneficial exercise.

In a biomotor ability analysis, you compare your current level of biomotor ability against a "gold standard" or perhaps a rival of yours that you wish to beat.

What is your biomotor ability?

As Bompa described in *Theory and Methodology of Training: The Key to Athletic Performance*, biomotor abilities are a collection of traits required in sport. These traits being:

- Speed
- Power
- Strength
- Agility
- Endurance
- Flexibility
- Co-ordination
- Balance

Each biomotor ability is scored against the gold standard for that ability. For example, for speed, the gold standard could be a 100-meter sprinter; for power, an Olympic weight-lifter; for strength, a power-lifter; for agility, perhaps a running back, or rugby winger. Rating your biomotor abilities is a mixture of art and science.

You initially start by scoring the gold standard for your sport (or particular rival). Once when working with a female downhill skier, we used Anja Paerson as the gold standard as she

Example 1: tennis player—gold standard, Roger Federer

BIOMOTOR ABILITY	OPTIMAL (FEDERER)	YOUR SCORE
Speed	9	6
Power	7	6
Strength	6	5
Agility	9	5
Endurance	6	5
Flexibility	8	5
Co-ordination	10	6
Balance	8	6
TOTAL SCORE	63	44

Example 2: golfer—gold standard, Tiger Woods

BIOMOTOR ABILITY	OPTIMAL (WOODS)	YOUR SCORE
Speed	9	6
Power	8	6
Strength	8	5
Agility	7	5
Endurance	5	5
Flexibility	7	5
Co-ordination	10	6
Balance	7	6
TOTAL SCORE	63	44

was the world number one and the client's rival. You then compare your own biomotor profile against the gold standard. Once you have completed the profiles for the gold standard or rival and your own, you then compare the sets of scores to see where the biggest deficits are. I have given two examples above making up sample scores. Note that only you and/or your coach can decide what scores are given.

As you can see in the table above left, if you scored yourself as I have suggested, then your biggest biomotor deficits would be agility and co-ordination (deficit of four points), followed closely by speed and flexibility (deficit of three points). While you would need to improve all biomotor abilities, the focus of your program would be on agility, co-ordination, speed, and flexibility.

As you can see in the table above right, if you scored yourself as suggested, then your biggest biomotor deficit would be co-ordination (deficit of four points), followed closely by speed and strength (deficit of three points). While you would need to improve all biomotor abilities except for endurance, the main focus for your own individual program would be on co-ordination, speed, and strength.

Instead of estimating the biomotor scores as suggested above, you can also use specific testing to test each biomotor ability. There are many tests available. I would suggest that if you are going to test yourself, make the testing process as close to your sport as possible, and where possible use the help of a strength and conditioning coach or a C.H.E.K practitioner.

MOVEMENT PATTERN ANALYSIS

As we learned in section two of this book, it is vital that we are able to perform Primal Pattern® Movements since they form the basis of all human movement, and therefore sports performance.

It is also important to remember that almost all movement patterns can be broken down into different segments of Primal Pattern® Movements. For instance, when someone throws a ball, they begin the movement with a lunge, then a twist, then a push to finish off.

A golf swing, for instance, requires a twist and a small degree of pull in the back swing, with a twist in the

opposite direction, a side lunge (lateral shift of the pelvis), and a degree of push on the downswing, and follow-through. A golfer will have to walk long distances, often over hills, bend down many times to line up putts, and pick the ball out of the hole. Therefore, a lunge and bend pattern would also be required in their program.

You need to consider which Primal Pattern® Movements are involved in your sport, and ensure that you perfect them before you move on to maximal strength, power, and speed training.

ENERGY SYSTEM REQUIREMENTS

The short-term system of energy production or "instant energy" is created by a substance called adenosine triphosphate (ATP). ATP is generated in the mitochondria of cells by combining adenosine diphosphate (ADP) and creatine phosphate (CP). There is initially enough ATP stored in the muscle for approximately five seconds of activity. For energy to be produced, one of the phosphate bonds breaks from ATP to form ADP + P. The cell then requires further CP to turn ADP back into ATP. However, there are only adequate stores of CP to maintain energy production for around 10 seconds. It can also take 30 seconds to replenish 50 percent of the stored CP, and up to two minutes for it to be completely replenished. For this reason, it is best suited to high-intensity, short-duration activity. Examples of these activities include

heavy weightlifting (90–100 percent of maximum effort), explosive reactions, shot putting, long jump, and sprinting.

The short-term energy system can be developed by using maximal strength (90–100 percent of 1 RM) and power-based training regimes. The short-term system is utilized during and at the start of an event, and to increase speed or climb a gradient during a race. If the intensity of activity continues for more than a few seconds, then another energy source must be used.

The system of energy production in the intermediate system is also known as the lactate system, anaerobic glycolysis, or the fast oxidative glycolytic system. This energy system uses glycogen (stored glucose from the liver and muscle tissue). The glycogen is broken down (glycolysis) when exercise is quite intense (60–90 percent of maximal effort), and for

longer than a few seconds. The glycogen breaks down within the cytoplasm of the muscle cell and converts to pyruvate to help produce ATP. This anaerobic metabolism of glucose produces more ATP than it uses. Some of the pyruvate breaks down into lactic acid (because no oxygen is present), which further breaks down into lactate and hydrogen. Lactate increases the acidity of the muscle, which inhibits some of the normal processes involved in muscle contraction. As intensity increases, the build-up of lactate is believed to be the cause of muscular fatigue and aching.

The intermediate system can last for up to three minutes, at which point the aerobic system becomes dominant with a decrease in intensity. It can take a few minutes to two hours to fully recover from the use of the lactate system. This system can be trained by using circuit training, short rest periods during resistance training, interval training, fartlek training, and long sprints. Type IIA muscle fibers are the predominant muscle fiber type used during activities using this system.

The system of energy production in the long-term system, or "aerobic energy," is the dominant energy source at rest, and during low-intensity activity such as endurance training (walking, jogging, and long-distance cycling). At a low intensity, the body can maintain an adequate supply of oxygen to the mobilizing muscles. ATP is produced by glycogen from the liver and muscles, and fatty acids from adipose tissue, subcutaneously, in and around organs, intra-muscularly, and from bone marrow. The glycogen and fatty acids combine with oxygen (beta-oxidation) within the mitochondria, which slowly produces ATP. The glucose (carbohydrates) and the fats are utilized at differing amounts depending on the intensity of the activity. The higher the intensity, the higher proportion of carbohydrates utilized, and the lower the intensity, the higher the proportion of fats utilized. The main waste products produced are carbon dioxide and water. These have little effect on muscular contractions, and the aerobic system is therefore a great source of energy for long duration activities. The aerobic system can be improved through steady low-intensity training. Type I muscle fibers are the predominant muscle fiber type used during activities using this system.

It is crucial that you train the appropriate energy systems required in the right proportions for your sport. The table (right) suggests energy source requirement for a number of sports.

Energy system requirements, referenced from M. Siff, *Supertraining*.

SPORT	SHORT-TERM SYSTEM % USED	INTERMEDIATE SYSTEM % USED	LONG-TERM SYSTEM % USED
Badminton	80	10	10
Baseball	80	20	0
Basketball	85	15	0
Cricket	80	20	0
Fencing	90	10	0
Field hockey	60	20	20
American football	90	10	0
Golf	95	5	0
Gymnastics	90	10	0
Ice hockey:			
Forward, defence	80	20	0
Goalie	95	5	0
Lacrosse:			
Goalie, defence, attack	80	20	0
Midfielders, man-down	60	20	20
Rowing	20	30	50
Rugby	90	10	0
Skiing:			
Slalom, jumping, downhill	80	20	0
Cross-country	0	5	95
Pleasure skiing	34	33	33
Soccer:			
Goalie, wings, strikers	80	20	0
Half-backs, link players	60	20	20
Squash	50	30	20
Swimming and diving:			
50m, diving	98	2	0
100 m	80	15	5
200 m	30	65	5
400 m	20	40	40
1,500 m, 1 mile	10	20	70
Tennis	70	20	10
Track and field:			
100 m, 200 m	95	5	0
400 m	90	10	0
800 m	30	65	5
1,500 m, 1 mile	20	55	25
3,000 m	20	40	40
5,000 m	10	20	70
10,000 m	5	15	80
Standard marathon	0	5	95
Volleyball	90	10	0
Weight-lifting	95	5	0
Wrestling	90	10	0

In sport and everyday life we encounter different surfaces that we must safely move over. In differing sports, or even within the same sport, such as triathlon and tennis, you may encounter different surfaces .

By the age of three we have developed most of our reflexes, which help prevent us from falling over and injuring ourselves. There are two main groups of reflexes. These are:

• Righting reflexes
• Equilibrium (tilting) reflexes

Righting reflexes are called into action to keep us from falling over when we are on predictable surfaces such as a basketball court, golf course, tennis court, baseball field, or athletics track.

Righting reflexes work via a complex system of assessment and action involving the head, neck, skin, and limbs to keep the body in a safe and correct position to complete a given physical task.

According to P. Chek in *Movement That Matters*, equilibrium reflexes include:

• Protective reaction of the arms and legs
• Tilting reactions
• Postural fixating reactions

There are a number of sports that require a combination of righting and equilibrium reflexes. However, most sports require dominance in one of the reflexes.

Equilibrium or tilting reflexes are dominant when the surface is unpredictable. Sports such as ice hockey, canoeing, surfing, horse riding, downhill skiing, and skateboarding use equilibrium reflexes more predominantly. It would therefore be advisable to train these reflexes in order to be successful.

There are a number of implements you can introduce to your training to train your equilibrium reflexes (see illustrations). These include:

• Swiss ball, also know as a gym ball, physio ball, or fit ball
• Stability disk
• Balance board
• Bongo board
• Fitter™
• BOSU

Making your exercises more unstable (as these implements do), may increase your likelihood of injury. You should begin this type of training at easy levels, and only progress the difficulty by small increments when you have mastered your current level.

If your sport requires you to have a lot of maximal strength, it is important not to spend too much time on this type of training, as it may reduce your peak strength.

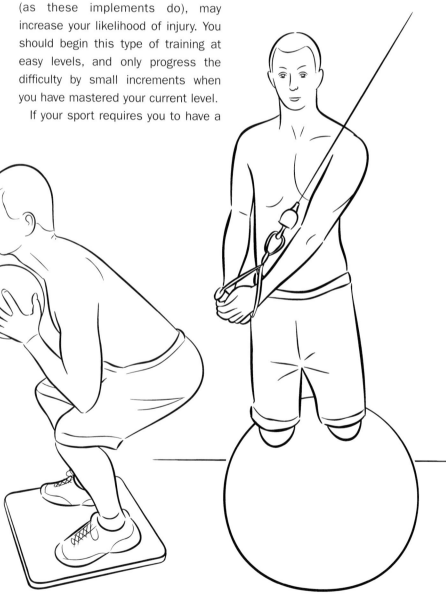

OPEN- VERSUS CLOSED-CHAIN EXERCISES

In human movement, and therefore in sport, movements can be open-chain or they can be closed-chain.

Open-chain movements occur when part of your body overcomes a load, be it gravity, a bat, a ball, an opponent, or a weight. For example, if your sport involves throwing a ball, your body and arm are able to overcome the load of the ball, gravity, and air resistance to launch it through the air. Similarly, if your sport requires you to kick a ball,

the same philosophy applies for the kicking leg.

Closed-chain movement occurs when you are unable to overcome a load, and you pull or push yourself across the object. For instance, a rock climber will push with their legs and pull with their arms to climb up a rock face. They cannot overcome the rock face, but they can move across it. Closed-chain movements also occur when you are walking and running.

When running, your propulsive leg drives into the ground and propels you forward. You aren't able to make the ground move, but you do move across the ground.

For your sport you need to assess whether you use open- and/or closed-chain movements, and in what proportions. You can then choose the correct exercises to condition your body effectively for your sport. For most sports, the upper body requires a predominance of open-chain exercises, and the lower body requires mostly closed-chain exercises.

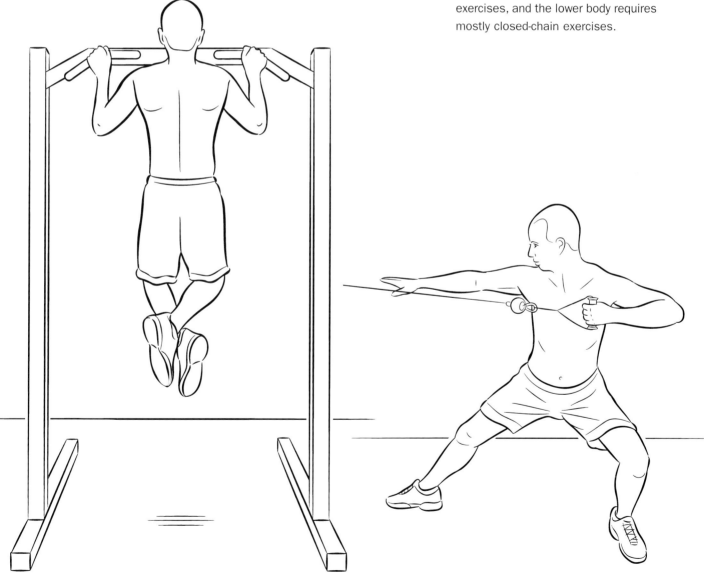

PERIODIZATION

Periodization involves the careful manipulation of exercise variables, and the gradual cyclical alteration of frequency, intensity, and volume of training throughout the year to ensure peak performance during the most important part or parts of a season. For some, this may be a world or national championship, or it may just be the maintenance of one's performance. For most, there is a distinguishable in-season and off-season.

Periodization is essential because peak performance cannot be maintained indefinitely, and focusing on just one biomotor ability throughout the year will leave you trailing your competition. If you try to develop all the biomotor abilities together, the gains you achieve will be negligible at best, and the likelihood of physical and mental exhaustion high. In addition, there is an inverse relationship between training volume and intensity. The more intense the training, the less you are able to handle without over-training. This is particularly important in-season, and especially if high-priority competitions are coming up. When coming up to big events, a good example being running a marathon, you need to taper your training. Tapering means a gradual reduction of frequency, volume, and intensity to give you optimal energy for the big event.

Each season can be separated into phases. The whole season is known as a macrocycle, and normally contains an off-season, pre-season, and in-season. A macrocycle can be as long as a four-year period if the sport is an Olympic one, for instance. Macrocycles can be divided into mesocycles, which are normally a series of weeks or months, and often focus on one strength quality, e.g. power, while maintaining gains made in previous phases, e.g. strength. Each mesocycle can be divided into microcycles. These normally involve the day-to-day plan of a training week.

Below is an example of a periodized training plan for a club level tennis player. It is by no means a plan for all tennis players—training history,

Example periodization plan of a club level tennis player—advanced athlete

	Oct			Nov			Dec			Jan			Feb			Mar		
Club tournament																		
Winter singles						X			X			X			X			X	
Doubles leagues																		
Training phase	Pre-season			Winter season														
Strength	Strength		Power	Strength		Power		Strength		Power		Strength		Power		Strength
Speed	Agility and plyometrics																	
Endurance																		
Macrocycle	1																		
Mesocycle	1		2		3		4		5		6		7		8		9	
Microcycle	1	2	3	4	5	6	7	8	9	10	11	12	13	14	15	16	17	18	19	20	21	22	23	24	25	26
Peaking index	4		3		4		3		4		3		4		3		4

	Apr			May			Jun			Jul			Aug			Sep		
Club tournament										X	X	X	X	X	X	X	X			
Winter singles			X																
Doubles leagues						X		X	X		X		X	X	X				
Training phase	Winter season		Off-season		Summer season										Off-season		
Strength	Str	Power	Strength		Power		Strength		Power	Strength	Power			Corrective	
Speed	Agility and plyo		Agility and plyometrics													
Endurance																
Macrocycle	1															
Mesocycle	9	10		11		12		13		14		15		16		17	18	19	
Microcycle	27	28	29	30	31	32	33	34	35	36	37	38	39	40	41	42	43	44	45	46	47	48	49	50	51	52
Peaking index	3	2		3		2		3		2		3		2	1	5	

biomotor abilities, competition schedule, and goals all need to be factored in. For the majority of the season, the player trains strength, power, agility, and plyometrics—high requirements for tennis. The main focus for the player is the club tournament, and you will see that she tapers her strength training for one week prior to the club finals, to be totally fresh. Hence, the "peaking index" of "1." The previous strength, power, and agility gained from the previous phases will easily last for that week. The season has also been divided into winter and summer, with two short off-seasons. The end of the summer is followed by a short rest, and then a corrective exercise phase to help correct tennis-specific muscle imbalances developed throughout the season.

Example of the microcycles: weeks 37–42

		MON	TUES	WED	THURS	FRI	SAT	SUN
Week 37 Build	A.M.		Strength: pull, twist—100% intensity	Agility & plyo: 120 foot contacts	Strength: lunge, squat—100% intensity	Agility & plyo: 120 foot contacts	Tennis with coach	Rest day
	P.M.	Doubles match/stretch	Stretch	Doubles practice/stretch	Stretch	Stretch	Singles practice + stretch	
Week 38 Build	A.M.	Strength: pull, twist—102.5% intensity + stretch	Agility & plyo: 140 foot contacts	Strength: lunge, squat—102.5% intensity + stretch	Agility & plyo: 140 foot contacts	Strength: pull, twist—102.5% intensity + stretch	Tennis with coach	Rest day
	P.M.	Stretch	Stretch	Doubles practice/stretch	Stretch	Stretch	Singles practice + stretch	
Week 39 Recover	A.M.	Strength: pull, twist—75% intensity + stretch	Agility & plyo: 80 foot contacts	Strength: lunge, squat—75% intensity + stretch	Agility & plyo: 80 foot contacts	Strength: pull, twist—75% intensity + stretch	Tennis with coach	Rest day
	P.M.	Stretch	Stretch	Doubles practice + stretch	Stretch	Stretch	Singles practice + stretch	
Week 40 Build	A.M.	Power: pull, twist—4 sets	Agility & plyo: 150 foot contacts		Power: lunge, squat—4 sets	Agility & plyo: 150 foot contacts	Tennis with coach	Rest day
	P.M.	Stretch	Stretch	Doubles match + stretch	Stretch	Stretch	Singles match + stretch	
Week 41 Build	A.M.	Power: pull, twist—5 sets	Agility & plyo: 170 foot contacts	Power: lunge, squat—5 sets	Power: lunge, squat—5 sets	Power: pull, twist—5 sets	Tennis with coach	Rest day
	P.M.	Stretch	Stretch	Doubles practice + stretch	Doubles practice + stretch	Rest	Singles practice + stretch	
Week 42 Recover	A.M.	Power: pull, twist—3 sets	Agility & plyo: 90 foot contacts		Power: lunge, squat—3 sets	Agility & plyo: 90 foot contacts	Tennis with coach	Rest day
	P.M.	Stretch	Stretch	Doubles match + stretch	Stretch	Stretch	Singles match + stretch	

REFERENCES

1. Chek, P., *The Golf Biomechanic's Manual: Whole in One Conditioning*, C.H.E.K Institute (1999)

2. Feldenkrais, M., *Body and Mature Behavior*, International Universities Press (1949)

3. Brandon, L. and Jenkins N., *Anatomy of Yoga for Posture and Health*, New Holland Publishers (2010)

4. Lee, D., *The Pelvic Girdle,* Churchill Livingstone (1999)

5. Bogduk, N., *Clinical Anatomy of the Lumbar Spine and Sacrum*, Churchill Livingstone (1997)

6. Gracovetsky, S., Farfan, H., and Lamay, C., *A Mathematical Model of the Lumbar Spine Using an Optimal System of Control Muscles and Ligaments*, Orthopedic Clinics of North America (1997)

7. Richardson, C., Jull, G., Hodges, P., and Hides, J., *Therapeutic Exercise for Spinal Segmental Stabilization in Low Back Pain*, Churchill Livingstone (1999)

8. Chek, P., *Scientific Core Conditioning* correspondence course, C.H.E.K Institute (1998)

9. Gracovetsky, S., *The Spinal Engine*, Springer-Verlag (1998)

10. Hannah, T., *Somatics*, Perseus Books (1998)

11. Gerwin, R., *Myofascial and Visceral Pain Syndromes: Visceral-Somatic Pain Representations*, Journal of Musculoskeletal Pain, Vol. 10, No. 1/2, pp 165–175 (2002)

12. Schmidt, R., *Motor Learning and Performance*, Human Kinetics (1991)

13. Chek, P., *Movement That Matters*, C.H.E.K Institute (2000)

14. Chek, P., *The Outer Unit*, (online) available at www.ptonthenet.com/displayarticle.aspx?ArticleID=102

15. Chek, P., *Back Strong & Beltless—Part 3*, (online) available at www.ptonthenet.com/displayarticleaspx?ArticleID=100

16. Newton, H., *Explosive Lifting for Sports*, Human Kinetics (2002)

17. Chu, D., *Jumping into Plyometrics*, Human Kinetics (1998)

18. Buckley, M. and Chek, P., "*CHEK Exercise Coach Certification Manual*," C.H.E.K Institute (2008)

19. Orietta, C. and Bompa, T., *Theory and Methodology of Training: The Key to Athletic Performance*, Kendall/Hunt Publishing Company (1994)

20. Siff, M., *Supertraining*, Supertraining Institute (2000)

GLOSSARY

Active closure is the stabilization of a joint created by myofascial (muscle and fascia) action. Often referred to in the stabilization of the sacroiliac joint.

Afferent nerves carry nerve impulses from receptors or sense organs toward the central nervous system. Also known as sensory nerves.

Compound exercise is a movement that involves a number of joints.

Contralateral refers to the opposite side.

Efferent nerves carry nerve impulses away from the central nervous system to muscles and glands. Also known as motor nerves.

Force closure is the stabilization of a joint created by myofascial (muscle and fascia) action. Often referred to in the stabilization of the sacroiliac joint.

Form closure is the stabilization of a joint created by articular components. Often referred to in the stabilization of the sacroiliac joint.

Hypertrophy is the increase in tissue size, often referred to as the increase of muscle tissue.

Intensity is a measure of load of an exercise relative to the current level of strength, often measured as a percentage of one repetition maximum (1 RM).

Ipsilateral refers to the same side.

Isolation exercise is a movement that involves one joint.

Muscle spindles are sensory receptors along the length of a muscle, which detect changes in the length of that muscle. Muscle spindles feed information back to the central nervous system.

Neural drive refers to the number and amplitude of nerve impulses received by a muscle.

Neutral spine is the natural position of the spine when standing without any muscle imbalances, and is achieved when the cervical, thoracic, and lumbar spinal curvatures each have an angle of 30–35 degrees.

Passive closure is the stabilization of a joint created by articular components. Often referred to in the stabilization of the sacroiliac joint.

Phasic muscles have a main role in creating movement across joints and gross stabilization of joints. They have a predominance of fast-twitch muscle fibers, can create high levels of force, are quick to fatigue, and tend to lengthen and weaken under faulty loading.

Reciprocal inhibition is a relaxation of a muscle on one side of a joint to accommodate a shortening of its antagonistic muscle.

Shear force is a parallel stress placed on a joint, often in an anterior–posterior or left–right direction. Shear occurs when an applied force produces sliding between two planes. Often referred to in relation to stress placed on the spine.

A **swiss ball** is an inflated PVC ball used for exercises. It ranges in size from 14–34 in (35–85 cm) in diameter.

Synergistic dominance takes place when a synergist muscle takes over the role of an inhibited prime mover muscle.

Tonic muscles' main role is in creating segmental stabilization of the joints. They have a predominance of slow-twitch muscle fibers, create low levels of force, are slow to fatigue, and tend to shorten and tighten under faulty loading.

Torsion is a rotational stress applied to an object. Often referred to in the rotational force (torque) placed on the spine.

Training volume is the combination of repetitions multiplied by the number of sets and weight (intensity) used over a period of time (workout, week, month).

Triple extension refers to simultaneous plantarflexion of the ankle with extension of the knee and hip joints.

Type I muscle fibers produce relatively low levels of force, contract slowly, are slow to fatigue, have a high number of mitochondria and myoglobin, and appear red in colour.

Type IIA muscle fibers contract relatively fast, and have a greater aerobic capacity than type IIB fibers, and take longer to fatigue. They have more mitochondria and myoglobin than type IIB fibers. They favour the lactate energy pathway, have a medium-sized diameter, and less propensity to muscular growth than type IIB, but more than type I.

Type IIB muscle fibers produce high forces quickly, are quick to fatigue, have a low number of mitochondria and myoglobin, and appear white in colour. Are also known as type IIX fibers.

INDEX

Page numbers in bold refer
to the glossary

A

"A" movement cone drill 96
abdominal stretches 32
abduction 17
absolute strength 23, 79
acceleration 79, 92
achievable goals 125
acromion process of scapula 14
active closure 54, **135**
adduction 17
adductor longus 11
adductor magnus 12
adenosine diphosphate (ADP) 130
adenosine triphosphate (ATP)
    130–1
advanced athletes, program
    design 124
aerobic energy 131
afferent nerves **135**
age 128
agility 22, 92
agility training 92

"A" movement cone drill 96
back-pedal-forward 100
biomotor ability 127
hexagon drill 93
lateral shuffle 101
loading parameters 125
180° turn ladder drill 94
square cone drill 99
"X" pattern multi-run cone drill
    98
"Z" pattern run cone drill 97
zig-zag crossover shuffle 95
alignment 21–2
alternate bounding with single arm
action 107
amortization phase 102
anaerobic glycolysis 130
anatomical planes 15
anatomical position 15
anatomical terms 16
anconeus 12
ankle movements 18, 20
ankling 113
ankling to sprint 121
"anterior" 16
anterior oblique system 53
arm swings 44
articular system 14
articulations 14
atlas 28

B

balance and alignment 127, 129
balance boards 130
ball exercises
    adductor stretches 36
    hamstring stretches 37
    lunge on ball 60
    seated cable pull 67
    wall squat 61
barbell exercises
    barbell back squat 81
    barbell bench press 84
    barbell lunge 80
    deadlift 65, 82
    Romanian deadlift 64
    single-leg deadlift 66
beginners, program design 124
bend and reach 41
bends
    deadlift 65, 82
    power clean 88
    Primal Pattern® Movements 55
    Romanian deadlift 64
    single leg deadlift 66
biceps brachii 10, 11
biceps femoris 12, 54
biceps femoris (long head) 12
biceps femoris (short head) 12
biomotor analysis 79, 92, 127
bones, typical features 13
bongo boards 130
BOSU 130
bounding
    alternate bounding with
        single arm action 107
    single leg bounding 108
box exercises
    front box jump 109
    jump from box 110
    side-to-side box
        shuffle 106
brachialis 11, 12
brachioradialis 11, 12

bracing technique 49
butt kickers 114

C

cable exercises
   seated cable pull 67
   seated cable push 72
   seated wood chop 75
   single arm cable pull 68–9
   single arm cable push 73
   single arm, single leg cable pull
      70–1
   single arm, single leg cable
      push 74
   single leg wood chop 78
   wood chop 76–7
calves stretches 38
cardiac muscle 10
carpals 14
cervical/thoracic mobilization 25
Chek, Paul 49, 55, 92, 130
chin-ups
   balance and alignment 22
   maximal strength 83
circumduction 18
clavicle 11, 14
co-ordination 127, 129
coccyx 14
complex training 102
compound exercise **135**
concentric strength 128
cone drill
   "A" movement cone drill 96
   back-pedal-forward 100
   lateral shuffle 101
   square cone drill 99
   "X" pattern multi-run cone drill
      98
   "Z" pattern run cone drill 97
contralateral **135**
coracobrachialis 11
core, inner unit 48–9

four-point tummy vacuum
   50, 125
   horse stance horizontal 52
   horse stance vertical 51
   loading parameters 125
core, outer unit 48, 53–4
coronal planc 15
cranium 14
creatine phosphate (CP) 130

D

deadlift
   intermediate deadlift 65
   maximal strength 82
   Romanian deadlift 64
   single-leg deadlift 66
deceleration 22
"deep" 16
deep longitudinal system 53, 54
deep muscles 11, 12
definitions 8–9
deltoid 11, 12
depth jump 111
diaphragm 48
"distal" 16
dumb-bell exercises
   front squat 62
   intermediate lunge 59
   push jerk 90
   Romanian deadlift 64
   single leg squat 63

wall squat 61
dynamic posture 21

E

eccentric strength 128
efferent nerves 135
elbow movements 19
endurance
   biomotor ability 127
   energy system requirements
      129
   speed endurance 22, 112
   strength endurance 79, 124
energy system requirements
   130–1
equilibrium reflexes 130
equipment 130
erector spinae 12, 54
exercise variables 124
   periodization 132–3
explosive start 92
explosive strength 79
extension 17
extensor carpi radialis brevis 11
extensor carpi radialis longus 12
extensor carpi ulnaris 12
extensor digitorum 12
extensor pollicis brevis 12
external oblique 11, 12

INDEX

F

falling starts 120
fascia 10
fast oxidative glycolytic system 130
femur 14
fibula 14
fit balls 130
Fitter™ 130
flexibility
  biomotor ability 127
  program design 124
  speed training 23
flexion 17
flexor carpi radialis 11
flexor carpi ulnaris 11, 12
flexor digitorum 11
force closure 53, **135**
forearm movements 18, 19
form closure 54, **135**
four-point tummy vacuum 49, 50
  loading parameters 125
front box jump 109
front squat 62

G

gait
  core 53–4
  Primal Pattern® Movements 55, 56–7
gastrocnemius 11, 12
gemellus inferior 12
gemellus superior 12
glucose 131
gluteus maximus 12
gluteus medius and minimus 12
glycogen 130–1
goal-setting 125
gracilis 11
greater trochanter 14
gym balls 130

H

hamstrings 54
  stretches 37
  walking hamstring stretch 42
heel kicks 47
heel strike 53, 54
hexagon drill 93
hip flexors stretches 35
hip joint 19

hip movements 20
horse stance 49
  horizontal 52
  loading parameters 125
  vertical 51
humerus 10, 14
hurdle exercises
  ankling to hurdle run-through to sprint 123
  hurdle fast legs 117
  hurdle run-through 119
  hurdle run-through to sprint 122
  single leg hurdle run-through 118
hydraulic amplifier mechanism 48
hypertrophy 23, **135**

I

iliac crest 14
iliopsoas 11
"inferior" 16
infraspinatus 12
integrated systems 14
intensity **135**
intermediate athletes, program design 124
internal oblique 11
intra-abdominal pressure 48
inverted bar pull 89
ipsilateral **135**
ischial tuberosity 14
isokinetic strength 128
isolation exercises **135**
isometric strength 128

J

joint movements 17–20
joints 14
jump lunge with twist 86
jump squat 87
jump training 102
jumps
  depth jump 111

front box jump 109
jump from box 110
jump squat 87
standing jump and reach 103
two-footed jumps ladder drill
    105

K
knee 20
knee joint 19
knees-up 46

L
lactate system 130
ladder drill
    ladder speed run 115
    ladder stride run 116
    180° turn ladder drill 94
    two-footed jumps ladder drill
        105
    zig-zag crossover shuffle 95
ladder speed run 115
ladder stride run 116
"lateral" 16
lateral rotation 18
lateral speed 22
lateral system 53–4
latissimus dorsi 11, 12
levator scapulae 12
ligaments 14
loading parameters 124–5
lumbar mobilization 27
lumbar rotations 33
lunges
    balance and alignment 21
    on ball 60
    barbell lunge 80
    intermediate 59
    jump lunge with twist 86
    lunge 59
    multidirectional lunges 43
    Primal Pattern® Movements 55
    split squat 58

M
macrocycles 132
mass 79
maximal speed 22
maximal strength 23, 79, 127
maximal strength training
    barbell back squat 81
    barbell bench press 84
    chin-ups 83
    deadlift 82
    loading parameters 125
    program design 124
    upper-cut squat 85
measurable goals 125
"medial" 16
medial rotation 17
median plane 15
medicine ball side toss 91
mesocycles 132
metabolic waste 24
metacarpals 14
metatarsals 14
microcycles 132–3
mobilizations 24
    cervical/thoracic
        mobilization 25
    lumbar mobilization 27
    thoracic mobilization 26
mobilizer muscles 22
Motor Learning and Performance
    (Schmidt) 55
motor programs 55–6
Movement that Matters (Chek)
    55, 130
multidirectional lunges 43
muscles
    energy system requirements
        130–1
    muscle attachments 10

muscle balance 21–2
    muscle spindles 102, 135
    muscular system 10–12
myotatic reflex 102

N
neck extensors 28
neck side flexors 29
needs analysis 126
neural drive **135**
neutral spine 21, 49, 50, **135**
Newton's second law 79

O
oblique stretches 31
occipital 28
open/closed chain exercises 131
open- versus closed-chain
    exercises 131
outcome goals 125

INDEX

P

Paerson, Anja 129
palmaris longus 11
passive closure 54, **135**
patella 14
peaking index 133
pectineus 11
pectoralis major 11
pectoralis minor 11
pelvic floor 48
pelvis 14

periodization 132–3
peroneus longus 54
phalanges 14
phasic muscles 22, **135**
physiological effects 124
piriformis 12
plantaris 12
plyometric training *see also* power training
  loading parameters 125
  standing jump and reach 103
plyometrics 23, 102
popliteus 12
"posterior" 16
posterior oblique system 53
posture 21–2
power 79
  biomotor ability 127
power clean 88
power leaks 57
power training *see also* pylometric training
  biomotor ability 127
  inverted bar pull 89
  jump lunge with twist 86
    jump squat 87
    loading parameters 125
    medicine ball side toss 91
  power clean 88
  program design 124
  push jerk 90
pre-event stretches 39–47
Primal Pattern® Movements 55–6
  bends 64–6
  loading parameters 125
  lunges 58–60
  movement pattern analysis 130
  program design 124
  pulls 67–71
  pushes 72–4
  squats 61–3
  twists 75–8
  wood chop 76–7

process goals 125
program design 124–5
  biomotor analysis 127
  energy system requirements 128–9
  movement pattern analysis 128
  needs analysis 126
  open- versus closed-chain exercises 131
  periodization 132–3
  reflex profiling 130
  strength qualities 126, 128
pronator teres 11
pulls
  chin-ups 83
  inverted bar pull 89
  Primal Pattern® Movements 55
  seated cable pull 67
  single arm cable pull 68–9
  single arm, single leg cable pull 70–1
push jerk 90
pushes
  barbell bench press 84
  Primal Pattern® Movements 55
  push jerk 90
  seated cable push 72
  single arm cable push 73
  single arm, single leg cable push 74
pylometric training
  alternate bounding with single arm action 107
  depth jump 109
  front box jump 109
  jump from box 110
  side-to-side box shuffle 106
  single leg bounding 108
  squat jump 104
  two-footed jumps ladder drill 105

Q

quadratus femoris 12

R

radius 10, 14
reactive speed 22
reciprocal inhibition 57, **135**
rectus abdominus 11
rectus femoris 11
reflex inhibition 48
reflex profiling 130
regional anatomy 15
regularly reviewed goals 125
relative strength 23, 79
repetition 124
rhomboids 12
rib 14
rib-cage muscles 48
righting reflexes 130
Romanian deadlift 64

S

sacroiliac joint 53, 54
sacrotuberous ligament 54
sacrum 14
sartorius 11
scapula 14
scapula movements 18
Schmidt, R. 55
seated cable pull 67
seated cable push 72
seated wood chop 75
semimembranosus 12
semitendinosus 12
sensory-motor amnesia 48
serratus anterior 11, 12
serratus posterior 12
shear force **135**
shoulder joint 19
shoulder movements 18, 19
side shuffle 45
side-to-side box shuffle 106
single arm cable pull 68–9
single arm cable push 73
single arm, single leg cable pull
    70–1

single arm, single leg cable push
    74
single leg bounding 108
single leg deadlift 66
single leg hurdle run-through 118
single leg squat 63
single leg wood chop 78
skeletal system 10, 13, 14
SMART 125
smooth muscle 10
soleus 11, 12
speed 112
    and acceleration 79
    biomotor ability 127
    classifications 22
    endurance 22, 112
    strength 79
speed training
    ankling 113
    ankling to hurdle run-through to
        sprint 123
    ankling to sprint 121
    biomotor ability 127
    butt kickers 114
    falling starts 120
    hurdle fast legs 117
    hurdle run-through 119
    hurdle run-through to sprint
        122
    ladder speed run 115
    ladder stride run 116
    loading parameters 125
    preparation 23
    single leg hurdle run-through
        118
spine/trunk movements 18, 20
split squat 58
sports energy requirements 131
square cone drill 99
squat push press 39
squats
    advanced 63
    balance and alignment 21–2

barbell back squat 81
    beginner 61
    front squat 62
    intermediate 62
    jump squat 87
    Primal Pattern® Movements 55
    single leg squat 63
    split squat 58
    squat jump 104
    squat push press 39
    wall squat 61
stability 23
stability discs 130
stabilizer muscles 22
stance phase 57
standing jump and
    reach 103

standing torso rotations 40
starting speed 22
static posture 21
sternocleidomastoid 11
sternum 11, 14
stiff-leg deadlift 64
stirrup bone 14

INDEX

strength 79 *see also* maximal
   strength training
   biomotor ability 127
   endurance 124
   qualities 126
stretch reflex 102
stretch-shortening cycle (SSC) 102
stretches
   abdominals 32
   adductors 36
   calves 38
   hamstrings 37
   hip flexors 35
   lumbar rotations 33
   neck extensors 28
   neck side flexors 29
   obliques 31
   pectoralis minor 30
   pre-event stretches 39–47
   tensor fascia lata 34
stretching 24
striated muscle 10
suffixes 9
superficial muscles 11, 12
"supine" 16
supraspinatus 12
surface of the sport 128
swing phase 57
swiss balls 130, **135**
synergistic dominance 57, **135**

T
tarsals 14
tendons 10
tensor fascia latae 11
teres major 12
teres minor 12
terminology 8–9
Theory and Methodology of Training 129
thoracic mobilization 25, 26
thoraco-lumbar fascia gain 48
thoracolumbar fascia 53, 54
tibia 11, 14
tibialis anterior 11, 54
tilting reflexes 130
timed goals 125
tonic muscles **135**
torsion **135**
torso rotations 40
training age 128
training experience 128
training volume **135**
transverse abdominus 11
transverse plane 15
transversus abdominus 48, 49, 54
trapezius 11
triceps brachii 11, 12
triple extension 135
trunk movements 18, 20
twists
   medicine ball side toss 91

Primal Pattern® Movements 55
   seated wood chop 75
   single leg wood chop 78
   upper-cut squat 85
   wood chop 76–7
two-footed jumps ladder drill 105
type I muscle fibers 124, **135**
type IIA muscle fibers 124, **135**
type IIB muscle fibers 124, **135**

U
ulna 10, 14
upper-cut squat 85
upper trapezius 12

V
vastus lateralis 11
vastus medialis 11
vertebra 14
visero-somato reflex 48

W
walking arm swings 44
walking hamstring stretch 42
wall squat 61
warm-up 24
weight and strength 79
wood chops
   seated wood chop 75
   single leg wood chop 78
   wood chop (intermediate) 76–7
wrist movements 18, 19

X
"X" pattern multi-run cone drill 98

Z
"Z" pattern run cone drill 97

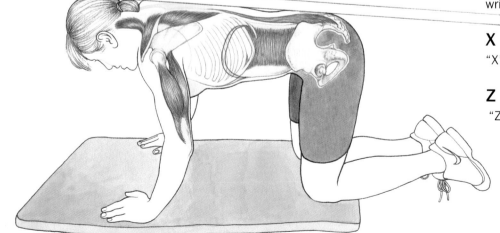

FURTHER READING

- Bompa, T., *Periodization—Theory and Methodology of Training,* Human Kinetics (1999)
- Brown, L. and Ferrigno, V., *Training for Speed, Agility, and Quickness,* Human Kinetics (2005)
- Chek, P., *Movement That Matters,* C.H.E.K Institute (2000)
- Chek, P., *Program Design—Choosing Reps, Loads, Tempo, and Rest Periods,* C.H.E.K Institute (2002)
- Chek, P., *Scientific Back Training— Correspondence Course,* C.H.E.K Institute (1998)
- Chek, P., *Scientific Core Conditioning— Correspondence Course,* C.H.E.K Institute (1998)
- Chek, P., *The Golf Biomechanics Manual,* C.H.E.K Institute (2001)
- Chu, D., *Jumping into Plyometrics,* Human Kinetics (1998)
- Knudson, D. and Morrison, C., *Qualitative Analysis of Human Movement,* Human Kinetics (2002)
- Newton, H., *Explosive Lifting for Sports,* Human Kinetics (2002)

USEFUL RESOURCES

www.bodychek.co.uk—the author's website containing articles, newsletters, a blog, online courses, live workshops, and resources to aid optimal health and performance.

www.chekinstitute.com—specialists in advanced education for health and fitness professionals, providing quality information, educational materials, and functional training tools.

www.nsca-lift.org—the professional body for strength and conditioning in the US. Members have access to research findings, techniques, up-to-date conditioning practices, and injury prevention methods. The NSCA is a resource for finding educational and training tools, and courses.

www.ptonthenet.com—member-based site for personal trainers containing articles, audio, and video from leading experts on health and performance.

www.uksca.org.uk—the professional body for strength and conditioning in the UK. Provider of workshops for professionals in strength and conditioning. The UKSCA also produces a quarterly strength and conditioning journal for its members and other resources availalble to purchase.

AUTHOR'S ACKNOWLEDGEMENTS

I would like to thank Paul Chek who has been the greatest influence on my career. Paul has been an inspiration, a teacher, a mentor, and a great friend. Without Paul's great teachings, this book would never have been written. I would like to thank my parents who have supported me throughout my career. Without their support, I would not be where I am today. To the guys at the UK Strength & Conditioning Association, thanks for your passion and drive to improve the standards of strength and conditioning. I really enjoyed your workshops—keep doing what you're doing. I would like to thank Ross and Sarah at New Holland for their support throughout the project. To James, whose artistic talent brings this book to life. I must also thank my clients and colleagues, past and present, for enabling me to develop and grow, and my friends for their support and for sharing many moments of laughter over the years.

Please note: the illustrations on pages 53, 54, and 55 are all adapted from original references by Paul Chek. Primal Pattern® is a registered trademark of Apriori Anatomikos Inc. and is used with permission.

La Porte County Public Library
La Porte, Indiana

More Anatomy for Strength and Fitness

Anatomy for Strength and Fitness Training
0-07-147533-8

Anatomy for Strength and Fitness Training for Women
0-07-149572-X

Copyright © 2010 New Holland Publishers (UK) Ltd
Copyright © 2010 in text: Leigh Brandon
Copyright © 2010 in illustrations: New Holland Publishers (UK) Ltd
Leigh Brandon has asserted his moral right to be identified as the author of this work.

First McGraw-Hill edition, 2010

10 9 8 7 6 5 4 3 2 1

All rights reserved. No part of this publication may be reproduced, stored in a
retrieval system or transmitted, in any form or by any means, electronic, mechanical,
photocopying, recording or otherwise, without the prior written permission of the
publishers and copyright holders.

ISBN   978-0-07-163363-5
MHID   0-07-163363-4

The advice presented within this book requires a knowledge of proper exercise form and
a base level of strength fitness. Although exercise is very beneficial, the potential for
injury does exist, especially if the trainee is not in good physical condition. Always
consult with your physician before beginning any program of progressive weight training
or exercise. If you feel any strain or pain when you are exercising, stop immediately and
consult your physician. As all systems of weight training involve a systematic
progression of muscular overload, a proper warm-up of muscles, tendons, ligaments,
and joints is recommended at the beginning of every workout.

This book does not constitute medical advice. The author and publishers have made
every effort to ensure that all information given in this book is accurate, but they cannot
accept liability for any resulting injury or loss or damage to either property or person,
whether direct or consequential and howsoever arising.

McGraw-Hill books are available at special quantity discounts to use as premiums and
sales promotions, or for use in corporate training programs. To contact a representative
please e-mail us at bulksales@mcgraw-hill.com.

Reproduction by Pica Digital Pte Ltd, Singapore
Printed and bound by Tien Wah Press (Pte) Ltd, Singapore